Potnia

A Devotional Anthology in Honor of Demeter

Edited by Melitta Benu
and
Rebecca Buchanan

Demeter by KS Roy

Copyright © 2014 by Neos Alexandria/Bibliotheca Alexandrina Incorporated

All rights reserved. No part of this book may be reproduced by any means or in any form whatsoever without written permission from the author(s), except for brief quotations embodied in literary articles or reviews. Copyright reverts to original authors after publication.

Dedication

For the mistress of good green growing things
And all those who celebrate and preserve her gifts

Invocation: Queen of the Universe

by Janine Canan

Heaven is hers, Earth is hers.
She is a warrior, She is a falcon,
She is a great white cow.

She fought the dragon and slew it.
She seduced the scorpion and tamed it.
The golden lion sleeps at her side.

She is the singer. She is desire.
She is the mountain of silver and gold and lapis.
On her hips tall trees grow, and grasses.

From Her, waters spout and savory grains.
Her lap is holy, her lips are honey,
her hand is law.

Her breast pours heavenly rain.
She is the healer. She is life-giver.
She is the terror, the anger, the hunger.

Fierce winds blow from her heart.
Hers is the thunder, the lightning, the glory.
She is the morning, She is the evening, She is the
    star.

She wears the gown of mystery.
Heaven is hers! Earth is hers!
Who can argue?

Table of Contents

Frontispiece: *Demeter* by KS Roy ... 3
Dedication ... 5
Invocation: Queen of the Universe
 by Janine Canan ... 6
Introduction and A Note on the Appendices
 by Rebecca Buchanan ... 13

Abandoned
 by Jen McConnel ... 16
Demeter, Waiting
 by Maya Spector ... 17
To Demeter Erinys
 by Jennifer Lawrence ... 18
The Crack
 by Janine Canan ... 22
Sonnet XV
 by Mike Alexander ... 23
[DeeDee in the Void]
 by John J. Trause ... 24
Aristi Chthonia
 by Michelle Auerbach ... 27
Tribute
 by Chryss Yost ... 29
Paleolithic Issues
 by Charles Stein ... 30
Demeter
 by Marian Weaver ... 35

Persephone's Lesson: Managing Terrible Truths
    by Marie Kane ... 37
Daughters of Demeter
    by Lauren C. Teffeau ... 39
Becoming Queen
    by Brandi Auset ... 47
Maiden in Love in the Underworld
    by Juli D. Revezzo ... 49
The Unexpected Visitor: A Modern Hellenic Tale of Winter Solstice Eve
    by Melia Brokaw ... 68
September
    by Dawn Corrigan ... 76
Seasonal Affective Disorder
    by Kim King ... 89
Let Winter Last for Aye!
    by Rosanna E. Tufts ... 90
Homecoming
    by Jennifer Lawrence ... 98
A Rose in Winter
    by Dana Wright ... 100
Letting Go
    by Gerri Leen ... 108
Pomegranate Cupcake
    by Erzabet Bishop ... 115
Through the Pain
    by Jen McConnel ... 124
Erysichthon
    by Kate Taylor ... 125

Demeter Melaina
    by P. Sufenas Virius Lupus ... 136
For Demeter
    by Jennifer Lawrence ... 137
Dem & I
    by C.D. Coss ... 139
Grain Mother
    by Jen McConnel ... 145
The Thrice-Ploughed Field
    by Suz Thackston ... 146
Harvest Prayer for Demeter
    by Melia Brokaw ... 150
Hymn to Demeter II
    by Rebecca Buchanan ... 151
Demeter's Kiss
    by Jennifer Lawrence ... 153
Demeter's Daughters
    by C.J. Prince ... 155
My Persephone
    by Jennifer Lawrence ... 157
Solstice Plea to Demeter
    by Melia Brokaw ... 159
Semolina Quinoa
    by Fern G.Z. Carr ... 162
Seeds
    by Rebecca Buchanan ... 164
Thalusia Hymn
    by Sannion ... 184
First Fruits Festival Prayer
    by Melia Brokaw ... 186

Song to My Mother
>by Janine Canan ... 187
Demeter's Lament for Demophoön
>by P. Sufenas Virius Lupus ... 188
Demeter's Other Children: Demophoön and the Eleusinian Mysteries
>by P. Sufenas Virius Lupus ... 190
Potnia-Ge (Our Lady of the Earth)
>by Katie Anderson ... 199
Hymn to Demeter Europa
>by Lykeia ... 201
An Ecstatic Prayer to Ceres
>by Christa A. Bergerson ... 203
Demeter Invocation
>by Romany Rivers ... 205
Eleusis Bound
>by Diotima Sophia ... 207
The Seed and the Fruit
>by John Opsopaus ... 209
Eleusinia Goetia
>by P. Sufenas Virius Lupus ... 257
Demeter and Goetia: The Eleusinian Mysteries and the Strange Case of Hadrian and Antinous
>by P. Sufcnas Virius Lupus ... 261
Mystery
>by Janine Canan ... 273
"The New Demeter": The Syncretism of Diva Sabina Augusta to Demeter/Ceres
>by P. Sufenas Virius Lupus ... 274

Prayer to Demeter
> by Hester Butler-Ehle … 282

Demeter
> by James Hall … 283

Appendix A:
The Homeric Hymn to Demeter … 284
Appendix B:
The Orphic Hymns to Demeter … 305
Appendix C:
Hymn VI to Demeter by Callimachus … 307
Appendix D:
Our Contributors … 310

About Bibliotheca Alexandrina — Current Titles — Forthcoming Titles … 329

Introduction
by Rebecca Buchanan

Demeter is a Goddess I have only lately begun to appreciate. As a child, I had little interest in food or agriculture. I certainly enjoyed eating (pizza especially), but no inclination to learn anything about where that food came from or how it was produced.

That changed after I found myself living on my own for the first time, having to pick out — and pay for — my own food. I suddenly became very aware of the cost of food, which in turn led to a growing curiosity as to its origins and production.

At the same time, my pursuit of a degree in women's studies led me to ecofeminism, which deals with the interconnections between women's rights, spirituality, and environmental issues. Ecofeminism, in turn, led me to Goddess Spirituality and a (renewed) interest in ancient mythology and Goddesses. Women, the Earth, mythology, Goddesses, agriculture: it all wove together, resulting in a very strongly nature-oriented Hellenic polytheism.

I was far from alone in my devotion to Demeter. As I discovered while assembling the many poems, short stories, plays, essays, and artwork for this anthology, though, people are drawn to Her for many different reasons. Some devotees see her as an aspect of the Great Goddess, the source of all creation. For others, She is part of a fluid trinity, encompassing the phases of a woman's life and the cycles of the year. Some devotees see Demeter as identical to the Roman Ceres, while still others consider them distinct entities. Some honor her as the Mistress of Good Green Growing Things, Lady of Herbs and Fruit, Queen of Flowers and Bees, She Who Bears the Golden Scythe, The Great Sow who taught us the use and preservation of seeds and who continues to bless our farms and gardens. Others experience her as the Law-Giver, whose gifts not only allowed humans to gather and thrive, but also necessitated the creation of customs and laws to ensure right behavior and the survival of civilization. For still other devotees, She is The Great Mother, The Destroyer, The Black Mare, Dark with Rage, Bringer of the Fallow Season, Mother of the Maiden who holds the world hostage until her daughter is returned. And for still others She is the Giver of the Mysteries, Overseer of Initiations, The Purifying One whose rites reveal secret truths and promise a blessed afterlife.

She is all of these, and so much more. She is Demeter, Goddess most worthy of our devotion.

A Note on the Appendices

For many people, the Homeric Hymn to Demeter is not only their first introduction to the Goddess, but also the basis for their understanding of and devotion to her. As such, a complete copy of that text — available through public domain — has been included in the first appendix. Additionally, two Orphic Hymns and a hymn by the Alexandrian poet Callimachus have been included. It is our hope that readers will find these works both helpful and inspirational.

Abandoned

by Jen McConnel

Alone in your pain,
you blighted the earth
for all the mortals who adored you
did not replace Her.

When springtime was gone,
you turned away your face
and left the men and beasts
to fend for themselves.

Until an old woman
unlocked your laughter
skirts lifted high
she reminded you
of the idiotic joy of life.

Demeter, Waiting

by Maya Spector

It is so much the daughter's story.
I recognize the truth of that.
But what of a mother's pain?
What is a woman to do with grief
for a lost child who is not dead?
What meaning does life hold for her?
I will tell you what she does.
She wanders aimlessly,
earth dry and dusty beneath her feet.
No color, no texture, no harmony now.
The aches of her aging body merge with
the pangs of her stricken heart.
Weight drags the body down
into leaden footfalls.
Surely there is some reason to go on.
It appears that life is for the young,
does it not?
Perhaps that is as it should be, but I,
I do have options to consider.
They say I must let go.
I recognize the truth of that as well,
but I will set the limits.
I am not yet
done with life.

To Demeter Erinys

by Jennifer Lawrence

Autumn is almost over, and the world inches on toward winter.
Day by day, the light fades, the earth grows colder,
And everything that once arched toward the sunlight
And flourished under my hands dies.
Apollo's light is thin and weak now,
And all the world senses the wrongness of your loss.

Demeter, I hear you weeping.

Mother bereft of child — a bargain was made,
But even though you agreed to it,
You mourn. What mother would not?
You think of her down there, cold and alone,
Sitting silent at the side of her dark groom.
Does he love her? Can he? As much as you do?
What man ever loved a woman so much as her mother does?

Demeter, I hear you weeping.

This is the time of hardship: ice thickly crusted in layers

Over everything, ground frozen to the bite of shovel or spade,
Leaves turned colors, curled, dry, and fallen underfoot to dust.
No thing grows. The animals that can flee the cold do,
Hastening to warmer climes. Those that cannot go stay behind
And suffer. And each man and woman wraps warmer clothes
Around themselves, curses the frigid chill, watches their breath
Steam in the air, and waits for winter to pass.

Demeter, I hear you weeping.

No solace to think she will return in a few months;
Each day apart is an agony, and the flowers refuse to bloom
At your bequest. No green buds bend the bough,
No fruit ripens, no velvet emerald grass to tread underfoot.
There is only the now of separation, the ever-present fear
And sorrow and rage. If your eyes must redden with tears,
Then so too will the world cringe and cower as sleet
Whips down from the heavens, coating all the world in ice,
Cold and impervious as your heart. Let Zeus know:

Until she is returned, there is only frost and death.

Demeter, I hear you weeping.

Lady of the Harvest, Mother of all things that grow,
Who would dare dream they have the right to command you
To dry your tears? Knowledge is no boon; even on the day
That she comes back to you at last, still the ember of grief
Burns bright in your chest, for you know already that
The days will pass, too swift for comfort or joy,
Before she must leave you once again.

Demeter, I hear you weeping.

Demeter, implacable one, unbending like the oak,
Sharp as the scythe that cuts down the grain,
You have shown them that even she of mildest seeming
Is not so easily cowed. Like a lion with her cubs,
You do not back down, nor stray from the path you have
Chosen for yourself. That greatest fruit you have brought
Out of your womb you protect, and in this neither
Wild Artemis nor battle-wise Athena may outshine your fury.

Demeter, I hear you weeping.

And I weep with you.

The Crack

by Janine Canan

When the flowering Earth cracked open and out
        charged
Hades, lord of the dead, to steal lovely Persephone,
daughter of Demeter, dragging her down
to his grim underworld, holding her prisoner
for thousands of years — it was the end

of loving, tending, and serving the Earth,
the beginning of man's rule over forest, desert,
ocean and sky, plant, animal, woman and child —
when the Earth cracked open and out charged
        Hades,
rebel son of Rhea, Mother of the gods.

<u>Sonnet XV</u>

by Mike Alexander

xv

To catch a snapshot of the virgin's face
her mother scans the missing persons files,
the girls who've disappeared without a trace,
the beatific eyes, the vacant smiles.
She's learning a new catechism, trials,
reprieves, a grief that cannot be controlled,
her daughter held by godless pedophiles
somewhere where innocence is bought & sold.
The days grow shorter, slowly turning cold,
as she exhausts the casebooks, one by one,
the trees outside the station turning gold,
then brown, & barren, until the day is done.
The roses by her bed refuse to bud;
She wakes to find her mouth half-full of blood.

[Author's Note: originally published in *We Internet in Different Voices* from **Exot Books**, 2008) .]

[DeeDee in the Void]

by John J. Trause

for Anne Carson

impulsa la soberbia el salto hacia el vacío

> Alí Chumacero Lora
> "El viaje de al tribu" (1958)

1

Spending her adolescent daughter's birthday in Georgetown on the telephone trying to get her [ex]husband in Rome to call [back], she leaves the door open, shouts, and cries, her daughter split in half across an ocean and time. Who left the window open? Did you see what she did?

2

Indigitamenta of [Demeter and] Ceres

Agnippe, "Nightmare"
Potnia, "Mistress"
Despoina, "Mistress of the House"
Thesmophoros, "Giver of Customs"

Erinys, "Implacable"
Chloe, "Green Shoot"
Chthonia, "She of the Ground"
Anesidora, "Sending up Gifts from the Earth"
Europa, "She of the Wide Eyes"
Kidaria, "She of the Tiara"
Vervactor, "(s)he who ploughs"
Reparator, "(s)he who prepares the earth"
Imporcitor, "(s)he who ploughs with a wide furrow"
Insitor, "(s)he who plants seeds"
Obarator, "(s)he who traces the first plowing"
Occator, "(s)he who harrows"
Serritor, "(s)he who digs"
Subruncinator, "(s)he who weeds"
Messor, "(s)he who reaps"
Convector, "(s)he who carries the grain"
Conditor, "(s)he who stores the grain"
Promitor, "(s)he who distributes the grain"

3

So the land grows dark, the dark earth rises
the pools turn to tarns and take turns, the cranes
fly past Hadley and Leeds, the dam bleeds out,
the shuttle from the looms scuttle no more,
there a half-built tree house above the flood
freezing, still almost

4

Leap into the void

[International Klein Blue]

into the [Artist's Shit]
into galleria Blu

into [pink]   [gold]

5

Pardon my fall, my fall, my slip, my fall,
but skiing's not for me or us.
I just want her back, my daughter.

NOTE: The epigraph may be translated, "Arrogance drives the leap into the void."

Aristi chthonia

by Michelle Auerbach

Six seeds and I still haven't spent the night but I can see it coming and I want to let that last blanket of snow cover the quiet for a while. I'm here where it's warm. My mother weeps for me, or she should. She weeps her mirror tears. Everything was up so close you could see the shine on her teeth.

I'm scared of you, but it's the vote up top that keeps me here, against both our vehement wills. It's okay, it's honkey dory, it's all what it is.

The old man told me to stop already with the too much. I can't tell you I'm not dangerous, that it's you I'm worried about. I can't ply you with the real questions. Who was the last lover? Was she here, like I'm here? Was it just for the bodies alive against each other, or is that now? Who was the woman in the green Cherokee on Tennyson Thursday night? Would I ever make you swear? Am I a detour on some trip around the afterlife? Who's got more to hide? Who wants to anymore?

I eat six seeds with quiet deliberation, feeling the skin pop and the astringent juice.

You can't answer any of my questions and I can't answer yours. Reach for me. Though I want to know how the seasons will spin and how she'll win me back, you might be for me. We'll see what happens.

Tribute

by Chryss Yost

I offer you these things, my living lord:
wildflowers baked in heavy bread,
a bouquet made of broken meadow birds,
a sculpture of the lovers' boats for rent
along the swirling edges of Charybdis —
one version of me waiting in each bow.

Uncarve me from this simple single skin,
your kisses, cupcakes hiding nail files,
the hinges from a dozen doors, and this
I offer you with open, floured hands —
to you, my purpose and my truest mate,
baking, waiting, lunging at the gate.

Paleothic Issues

by Charles Stein

The overwhelming grief of Demeter affects us with the full human pathos of a mother's loss of a beloved child. One feels in Demeter the single mother, bonded with her adolescent daughter, her anguish when that daughter is kidnapped, raped, murdered. But what does it mean for a universal figure like Demeter to feel such anguish? Since her universality, as goddess of nature's abundance, straddles two human epochs — one where men and women hunt and gather the freely given fruits of Demeter's bounty (an epoch that stretched over 99% of the existence of our species); and the other, where agriculture organizes sustenance, wealth accumulates in the hands of the few, and the hierarchical State enforces the toil of the many — is there perhaps some connection between this double reign and the nature of her anguish?

Marshal Sahlins in *Stone Age Economics* demonstrates that Paleolithic hunters did not live in scarcity, but abundance and leisure, interpretation of the data to the contrary betraying the prejudice of a later age; nor were hunting people shorter-lived than any later humans until the mid 20th century.

Peter Lamborn Wilson, in *The Shamanic Trace* remarks: "[A] great mystery hovers around the question of agriculture: — what on earth could induce any sane person to give up hunting and gathering (four hours daily labor or less, 200 or more items in the 'larder'...) for the rigors of agriculture (14 or more hours a day, 20 items in the larder, the 'work ethic,' etc.)?...A study of myths and folk tales about the origin of agriculture reveals over and over again that it was an invention of women — and the establishment of agriculture somehow entailed violence to women (sacrifice of a goddess, for example)."

What if the Demeter/Persephone story amounts to this: Demeter delivers agriculture to men through Triptolemos. Persephone, the gathering maiden, must be raped, abducted, delivered over to male control. Then Demeter's grief and rage is not over the loss of her daughter only, but harbors a trace of a far vaster and more general anguish — that of the entire human race's loss of its primordial autonomy and happiness to the power of authority and the state.

Wilson does not argue for the innocence of the tribal community, quite the contrary. He recognizes that the possibility for the concentration of wealth and power in the hands of a few must have been born with the emergence of homo erectus as a tool-using creature. Rather, tribal institutions were formulated very early to prevent the actualization of this possibility. The Neolithic revolution and the appearance of agricultural, hierarchical, city-centered civilization, perhaps around 10,000 B.C. in Jericho or Catal Huyuk represent the failure of these ancient institutions. Every civilization valorizes its conquest of the autonomous, egalitarian mentality of the tribe in myths that tell of the subjugation of the wild. Gilgamesh tames his wild-man friend-to-be, Enkidu; the Tibetan Buddhists enlighten the savage Bon; Christians convert or slaughter pagans; Olympians triumph over Titans; and the business goes on today every time the WTO or the IMF or Morgan Chase imagines it is doing an "undeveloped nation" a favor by forcing its participation in the global economy.

Wilson speaks of "the cruelty of agriculture ('raping the body of our Mother Earth' as hunters often call it). In tense anxiety about the calendar, the seasonal year .. which must be adjusted to 'fit' the astral year (the image of divine perfection), leads to a view of time as 'cruel.' The smooth time of the nomadic hunter ... is replaced by the grid-work, the cutting of earth into rigid rows, the year into layers, society into sections ... The farmers who work fourteen hours a day instead of four are being cruel to themselves; logically then they will be cruel to each other."

The planter must grow anxious about the yield of the land, the efficacy of his technique, the efficiency of his laborers. The first tract on the work ethic is actually written by Hesiod: his poem called *Works and Days* is an extended rant at his n'er-do-well brother on the consequences of laziness to the farmer. Hard work is treated as a good in itself. It is not enough that poorly tilled land causes the land to yield poorly: the gods punish the lazy farmer with the failure of his crops. The Protestant ethic and its twisted metaphysics is spelled out two thousand years in advance in all the starkness of its cruelty and irrationality.

The link between Hades and Ploutos becomes somewhat clear. In tribal society accumulation of wealth is moderated by rituals and customs of redistribution. The chief may gather great quantities of yams or pigs, "but is also obliged to beggar himself by giving feasts...."

Wealth that remains centralized and accumulated in an individual or a class must wait for a mode of manipulation of nature where there can be a surplus in one place — the banks or stock piles of the wealthy — and therefore scarcity in another — the poverty of the peasants or the workers or, in our world, the industrial nations' monopolization of resources and the third world's debt. In the world of hunting and gathering there is neither surplus nor want, only abundance or dearth, in the existential present. Wilson traces the development of wealth as parallel to the development of writing and money, the latter being the capacity to represent wealth that then allows, magically, the representation to *be* wealth. Another parallel exists in language and writing's relation to the sacred through holy writ: the power of speech to symbolize the sacred becomes the sacred itself. The temple priests of civilization who know the representations of the gods and spirits and thus monopolize and mediate their being, creating as it were a surplus and scarcity of sacred substance, contrast with the tribal shamans and medicine men who make the spirits to appear in themselves.

Here we see the peculiar place of Eleusis, which finds itself, like its goddess, Demeter, straddling the agrarian and a more ancient sacrality. The Hierophant, as his name implies, was closer to the shaman than to the priest, in spite of the well-established role of the cult over which he officiated. It was his job to allow "the holy things" of Demeter to appear, and, in the existential present of the final moments of the Mysteries, to avail the people in attendance of the spirits and gods themselves, not mediate their representations merely.

Though the Mysteries served Athens, the Mystery they vouchsafed bespoke another reality than the social complex that supported the Athenian State, for the Secret Itself undoes hierarchy, even as it is harbored in its midst. It liberates the individual spirit from the life of anxiety and subjugation (or mastery) that masters everyone under the civilized regime.

Demeter

by Marian Weaver

I cannot touch you,
Yellow-haired lady crowned with flowers,
Kissed by the sun.
I am in your shadow.

Was it narcissus your daughter picked
when she was dragged from the light?
Irony.
Your screaming drowned out hers
and every eye was on you.
It was all about you.
It was only, ever, about you.

I cannot pity you, lady,
With your torn clothes and furrowed cheeks.
You wail for yourself.
Comfort me, you beg — and I cannot.

You are every mother of every disappeared girl,
Standing on your doorstep with your please, please,
    come home,
Granting exclusive access for the interview,
Surrounded by a carefully landscaped meadow of
    photos,
Telling stories of your grief,
Making a gift of your tears — again — to your rapt
    audience.

You devoured your daughter.
Her tragedy was your balm.
It kept you alive while you starved the world.

I cannot weep with you, cannot worship you, lady,
Though I, too, am a mother with lost daughters.
I learned to weep in darkness and suffer without
    words.
I learned how to disappear, so that the world would
    remember them —
Because I, too, was once a lost daughter,
And my mother's shadow still falls over me.

I do not know you.
I will never know you.
I am nothing like you.

Persephone's Lesson: Managing Terrible Truths

by Marie Kane

Why do you hate your dear mother?
my therapist asks.

*If I hate Demeter, it's for the wreck
of an earth she created after Hades'
horses reared and his arm crushed
my breast as he took me,*
I reply.

*The barrenness, the parched earth,
the wicked storms, the lives lost,
and her wailing through it all
as she punished Earth's canvas,*
I say.

We walk a trail that climbs
to a spine of lifted rock
that peers over a fine web
of showy trees offering
their vivid leaves
to the wind.

When third solstice comes,
she asks, *what zigzag bolt
of force from you will compel
these leaves to loosen,*

drop to the ground,
and be interred
under snow and ice?

When I do not speak, she replies,
Perhaps, Persephone,
even immortals despise
what they already recognize.

Daughters of Demeter

by Lauren C. Teffeau

I.
"When famine snared our bellies, when it addled our minds and made us monsters, Mother Goddess came and bargained for our salvation. How could we not agree? How could we measure one life equal to that of the village?"

That is what the sibyl tells us around flame-lit circles. Even though that is exactly what the Mother had done.

My sisters before me left us as girls after the harvest. The sibyl says they come back as women, each spring. But I've seen the pale cheeks, mouths the color of old blood, hands that flutter at their sides as if to ward off the sunlight. They are hollow vessels, stripped of name and family. And none of our men will have them. At night, when the candle burns low, I ask the Mother why, but she never answers.

I witnessed a Claiming once, two seasons past, from behind the mask of a stag. Counted my breaths until he appeared, casting day into shadow.

My sister before me shuddered. But our lord never looked at her. His eyes were only for the head priest who shoved her forward. "You know the price for your complicity in the Mother's schemes."

The priest fell to his knees as if struck down. Then my sister vanished with our lord, but not before his eyes found mine.

The desolation and anger I saw in his gaze that day is my only comfort as the priests hold me under. My skin smarts where they abraded it with soap, cloth, brisk hands. Where they sloughed away who I used to be. I'm only allowed to scream when I'm underwater — the sibyl told us that's the only acceptable time to rid ourselves of the injustice that poisons us. When the fight leaks from my frame, when the last of my breath bubbles out, when I'm finally lifted from the pool, I am no longer me.

I'm declared ready. Incense burns the air. Pomegranate oil is massaged into my hair. Honey and cream, my skin. By hands gentler now with assurance I won't run. Scented oil anoints my forehead, my neck, my breasts. The inside of my elbows and knees. I burn with life for one lonely moment before they drape my body with linen, extinguishing all sensation. It is time.

I keep my eyes lowered, as a demure maiden should. Then shadow falls, announcing our lord. Fingers burn along my chin as my head is forced up to face him. I thought there would only be coldness in the dark, but I was wrong.

He has no words for the priest this time. A hand at my elbow, one at my back, he is all courtesy as we descend. "Do you know why you are here?"

"No, my lord."

A growl edges his voice. "It is always the same."

Hours, days later he says to me, "The Mother loves too fiercely. Though not the ones she uses so poorly." He reaches out, and the heat of his hand buffets my cheek as he fingers my hair. "Though you are not afraid."

II.
I blink back brightness, adze sharp.

Nettles burn my skin wherever the priest and the sibyl touch me as they lead me back to the convent. My sisters before me wait in welcome. I was lost for a long time, they tell me. I only know this harsh world requires too much of myself to navigate it. My sisters with their sad faces say it gets easier. I can only marvel at their lies.

Old sibyl gives me queer looks when she visits with me each afternoon. Asks me how I feel, if I need anything. But I don't know what I need. That must be why I feel this way. An unperson. No longer a girl, but a woman neither.

I walk sometimes. Leave my sisters behind and wander. It's the only time I can rid myself of the wrongness that whispers around me on the breath of the trees. I stay away from the herds of goats and sheep blanketing the hills, as they scream and bleat whenever they spy me or my sisters.

As the summer sun hangs overhead, I rest in a sweet-smelling field. White flowers cushion my body, one arm supporting my head, the other draped over my eyes. Then the sun vanishes, a warm hand cupping my cheek. I open my eyes and sit up, but there is only darkness. But it doesn't hurt, not like the light does.

"You said you would not forget. You promised. You are the only one who can stop this." The voice tugs something loose in my chest. I reach out, but the sunlight returns. Along with the pain, crowding out all thought.

It takes me too long to learn nighttime is easier. My mind clears enough to remember I was different once. Heat still drenches the air when I leave my chambers and walk out under the moonlight. I sit along the fountain, star-kissed ripples radiating from my fingertips. But I am not alone.

"She's remembering." Old sibyl's voice is harsh in the night. "Maybe he — "

"What would our lord want with her? She's no different from her sisters and the Goddess before her," says our priest, brandishing a candle against the dark. "Let us wait a while longer before — "

Bile collects in my throat. I am different. I—

The sibyl draws up to her full height. "I have been charged with this task by powers greater than you, priest. Prepare the draught. There can be no mistakes."

Mistake. Is that what I am? But then I remember the voice, the rightness I felt in that brief moment at the field. Rightness I have never felt behind the convent walls. I know that much.

Tears sting my cheeks at the thought of abandoning my sisters. I ask the Mother for guidance but she remains ever silent. When alarms ring out that I am no longer abed, I pad barefoot beyond the gates, down the road, to the forest.

I don't look back.

III.

A stick lodges in my side. I crawl out of my nest of leaves at the base of a tree and find an old woman staring down her cane at me. "What business do you have in these woods?"

I had traveled much of the night, searching for the field where I first heard him, hoping to learn more. But only silence and a chilled wind greeted me. So I returned to the forest, taking comfort in the shadows, and walked until I could go no further.

I hold out my hands. "I'm lost and I cannot return from where I came."

"Cannot or will not? Come with me, child. Old granny will see to you. Then we shall talk."

Her hut is not far, and soon a mug of tea warms my hands as we sit by her small fire.

"There, there, child. Now tell me why you cannot go home."

"Another home, another life, waits for me underground."

She cackles. "You're too pretty to live with the moles."

I shake my head. "No. I would live with our lord in the land below." It was his voice calling to me — I know that now.

The old woman hisses. "You? When that impertinent brat already claimed the Goddess's own?"

"But I must find a way to return. If I can, we...." It's still hazy but I'm certain of one thing. "He would claim her no longer."

The old woman throws down her cane, casts aside her bonnet, gray hair now golden in the firelight. "You consider yourself better than my daughter?"

My mug falls to the floor. I press my forehead to the packed dirt of her hearth. "Mother Goddess, I — "

"Silence. You have prayed at my altars, you took your place in the bargain I struck. And now you would destroy — "

I raise my head, but my voice is raw. "I would go back. For him. He needs me."

The Mother is the one who hid her daughter away from the world, compelled our village to fulfill the bargain she made with our lord. She forced him to accept my sisters, so ill-suited to life underground, as substitutes for the one he could never have lest he see her destroyed. He has remained trapped in his realm ever since except for those moments when he returns my sisters to the world of the living, emptied of the life that once defined them. But somehow I am still me.

The Mother may have been the one who created the void in the land below. But I will fill it.

"He has corrupted you." Cold hands lift me from the floor. The Mother Goddess's all-seeing eye on me. But I am blinded as tears course down my cheeks. "I cast you aside. You are no daughter of mine. Do what you will."

The hut melts away, the Mother with it. I'm left standing at the edge of a muddy lake, a forlorn place where no bird calls. My gaze is drawn to a rocky slope, a dark shadow cleaving it in two. The cave compels me forward.

I walk for millennia, down and down, the darkness my only companion. But I already feel more like myself.

I remember how man and beast alike answered my summons into death and darkness, a feat none of my sisters could manage. I remember the sorrow in my lord's eyes when Spring came, my promise to find a way to return, unfettered by the Mother's schemes. I remember the ache in my chest, the disorder of my mind, when his hands were replaced by old sibyl's. She held back my hair as I drank her foul potions, told me I was safe, that I would forever be the Mother's chosen. But she never told me what I had lost.

He is waiting for me when I cross the river. A disbelieving sort of joy on his face, so familiar I wonder how I could have forgotten it so long.

The Mother Goddess keeps the world in balance above even though no more of my sisters descend for their six months in hell. I take their time gladly, forever at my lord's side in shade.

Becoming Queen
by Brandi Auset

Does he treat you well
my mother asks
when you're in the dark

and what am I to say
to speak the truth
negates her wailing
belittles the pain caused by an endless winter
and the lives lost in pursuit of me.

Like all she's made
I longed to grow and be free.

Should I tell her
of how the sulphur smell of him rose from the roots
of the trees
would she understand the heat
of the fires
that kiss my toes as he caresses my instep.

How to say
that I called and he came.

So I remind her
that I am blood of her blood
power of her power
magick of her magick
I hint of how Grandmother
teaches me the craft of the hounds and the moon
I speak of spring
our time together
Mother and Daughter, in fields of her creation.

She hands me baked grains and honeycomb
these sweet pieces of her heart
and I accept them gratefully
tucking deep inside me
that I wasn't so much stolen
as tempted.

Maiden in Love in the Underworld

by Juli D. Revezzo

Ceres stood at her cottage window. Outside her beautiful gardens, the whole of the landscape was dying. Sacred sacrificial fires burned unceasingly within the temples; the populace clamored from Sicily to the Alps, and yet, she heard none. Their prayers fell on the goddess' ears, deaf to all but Proserpine's cries. The girl's pitiful, horrified screams burned in her heart even now.

Ceres had spared nothing in her rescue; she'd searched high and low, for months on end. Each night she lit torches at the fiery mouth of Mount Aetna to light her persistent search throughout mighty Rome, Greece, the golden fields of countries yet unknown. All she found of her beloved Proserpine was her beautifully woven sash, given to her with a sorrowful tale by a heartbroken dryad. With this, Ceres charged up Mount Olympus and confronted the gods, demanding retribution.

It seemed they knew the tale all too well, for Jove took her aside and gave her the awful news: Pluto, stricken lovesick by those fiends Venus and Cupid, had taken her beloved Proserpine into his dark underworld, foolish, desperate to make her his queen.

They warned Ceres she must heed their wishes. Her people suffered, she must relent, they said.

No; she would not. Rage burned within her as she paced her cottage. Visitors came, begging her to rethink her decision. She turned them all away. Yet, Mercurius returned, repeatedly, trying to dissuade her.

"Mercurius — " She rounded on the god, and waved a testy hand toward Jove's palace. " — remind them, if they must be reminded. Unless Proserpine is returned to me, safe and whole, the world will die."

"But my Lady!" he protested. "You must see reason. You simply cannot allow this to be. Please — "

She refused to repeat herself. "You have my decision. Take that to His Damnedness. Lay the blame on him. He releases my daughter, or else." She pointed to the cottage door and crossed her arms, shutting down behind them. "Go."

Mercurius opened his mouth to argue, but Ceres gave him a stare as fiery as the mountain, even though her eyes held ice in their emerald hue. Mercurius sighed, bowed and off he went.

She sighed. Months ago they had been happy. Proserpine was an innocent maid; nothing hindered her care, her warmth, her wonder in the face of the world's gifts, and Nature responded in kind.

It was her own fault, Ceres thought, that Proserpine had been kidnapped. She'd not kept a closer eye on the maid. What kind of Mother was she to allow this to happen?

It was not her fault — no. She'd done everything she could to protect her child.

Were it not for Venus and her scheming ways, not for crafty Cupid, or Pluto and his wandering eyes and greedy, grasping hands, Proserpine would be with her, and all would be well. But why Proserpine? Pluto was full of pure mischief, plain and simple. He was doing this out of spite, and until he felt the sting as deep as had she, Nature would remain in hibernation.

Mercurius returned, announcing Jove had summoned her.

"No!" she answered to the Sky Father's demands. How many times must she say it? In how many languages? "I will not relent until she's returned. You have my decision."

Jove sighed. "I cannot force him, Ceres. He would make her a fine husband, and you and I a fine son-in-law. Take that to heart, and do your duty. You mustn't allow our people to suffer. Please, see reason."

"There is no reason without Proserpine, and there will be no life, either." Ceres barely contained her ire as she returned home. What did they expect? She must remain firm, determined. She couldn't let Pluto win!

She only wished she knew how to reach her daughter. Sighing, the goddess stared across the landscape to her temple in Enna, longing. Proserpine, her heart cried, return to me!

***

Proserpine wandered the market, alive with enticing scents of all kinds, and rowdy, joyous sounds. Yet she couldn't share their joy. Pluto had taken her without her leave, tried to win her heart, bade her settle in his dark world as he wished. He gave her everything she could want, anything to see to her comfort, insisted this was her home. The land was in fine bloom, the market noisy, full of song and conversation, cries of the merchants added to the din. They each offered her delights, cakes, fine clothing fit for a queen. Yet, no matter what they offered, Hades would never be her home. She craved true fresh air, warm sunlight, colorful, sweet flowers, majestic oaks, willows, pine, soft grass beneath her feet. She missed the fields and streams, and especially her beloved mountain!

She picked up a beautiful gold necklace, running its soft cold links through her fingers before she dropped it back to its case. Something niggled at the edges of her memory: A dark river, the laments of the dead, twisting tunnels that led nowhere. Outside this dream, Pluto's world, in fact, seemed filled with darkness. This beauty was illusion, an imitation he painted for her. Wasn't it?

And what she heard of the world above! It was enough to make a serene Lady like herself, mad with sadness and fear. How could her mother allow such an act? She had tried — oh, she had tried many ways to escape, to tell her mother she need not lament; that she was safe.

Sick in heart and body, Proserpine sunk down to a colorfully woven rug, gaining a welcoming nod from the nearby rug merchant, before he turned back to his work. Dismissing her as she sat there sulking.

A tear slipped down her cheek.

"What is the matter, my love?"

Startled by the deep voice, Proserpine looked up.

He stood before her, Pluto. Dread King of the Underworld. His dark eyes studied her and she could see concern written in them, but she was unmoved. "Go away."

He offered his hand. "Come now, love, don't sit here in the shadows and brood. It's not good for you."

"Why shouldn't I? That's all you have here: shadows."

Pluto's dark brow rose. "Is it?" He peered upward, shading his eyes from the muted sun. "I see no shadows here. Phoebus's sun burns as bright as ever, and warm." He knelt down beside her, nudged a lock of hair out of her eyes with a gentle touch. "Step out from your hovel. You'll see."

Proserpine couldn't be sure, but she thought her heart melted a little at the tender gesture.

He took her cold hands in his, pulled her to her feet, and led her through the market. She gazed upon the beautiful gold and bone necklace she had coveted earlier. Pluto picked it up in his strong hands. "Do you like this?" he asked.

She bit her lip, afraid she might say the wrong thing.

A tender smile curled his lip, and he circled her, leaned into her from behind. His warm breath tickled her ear. "Then you shall have it." He reached over her head, dangled the necklace before her eyes. The little pomegranate pendant glinted in the sun like fire opal yet the rind, the bulbous point at the end, seemed as supple as the real fruit.

The chain, and his fingers, slide across her skin and Proserpine shivered. The clasp slid into place, the pendant fell against her chest with a soft thunk.

"Come." He scooped her up in his arms, causing her to laugh, and carried her to his chariot.

His horses galloped at a breakneck speed through the underworld until they paused in a peaceful meadow. Before them, the branches of a great olive tree wafted in the warm breeze; birds twittered overhead. She heard a brook babbling in the distance. Mount Aetna stood before her, majestic, silent. Proserpine gasped in surprise.

She took another deep breath. The air was sweet and smelled of crocuses and violets.

When had they returned home?

Pluto settled down beside her. Out of the corner of her eye, she noticed him watching her. She smiled and plucked a violet from the grass, running her fingers lazily over its petals. She felt a light touch tickle across her forearm, and she looked over. He was studying her intently. "Tell me what you love."

Heat blazed up her cheeks, and she brought the flower to her nose, to hide the flush. "This." Underlying the violet's familiar sweetness, there was a hint of something strange, something old, dried, decaying. Proserpine wrinkled her nose, sneezing the undertones away. She offered him the flower. "This is what I love."

His dark curls wafted in the breeze as he leaned forward to sniff. His beard tickled her fingers. "Lovely." The delicate violet's petals grazed his nose and the flower withered. "Absolutely beautiful."

She blinked. "Beautiful?" She could see nothing beautiful in the drooping head.

Pluto shrugged. "Well, before it died? Such is life, Proserpine, don't you agree?"

She frowned down at the withered treasure, caressed the brittle petals. They bloomed again with vibrancy and color. She sighed as she lowered the flower to her lap. "Would that I could do that with everything here."

"You have." He stroked a finger down her cheek. "You have, more than you know. For which I would gladly spend forever repaying you."

She shaded her eyes from the sun. The landscape seemed so much like home. Could this be true? The stories she'd heard about Pluto's home hadn't come close to reality. It was a warm realm of light and beauty. The god himself didn't fit the tales. He was sweet, and kind.

"If you will be my queen." He took and kissed her hand, a light brush of his lips across her knuckles.

A thrill ran through her, followed by fear. She dipped her head, her hair falling across her face like a veil.

Had he really suggested what she thought? Is this, then, what he'd been leading up to? Proserpine scanned the landscape, wishing she could consult her friends, her mother. Could she really accept his offer without their counsel?

Could she love the man behind the awesome power? The one that made humans the world over quake.

Looking into his soulful, expectant dark eyes, there was only one answer.

He kissed her hand. "Well?"

Yes. It was time, she realized, to grow up. To do what she'd always hoped she could do. Shyness flamed in her and she nodded. "I think I'd like that."

"Do you really?"

She nodded once again, fondling her bone necklace. "If you love me."

"You have no idea how much." He wrapped her in his warm embrace, lips brushed across hers. The kiss sent her head spinning, filled her senses with sweetness, and a hint of ash. He pushed her back slightly and swiped a blonde curl from her forehead. An impish grin lit his handsome face. "Now, what are we going to tell your mother?"

***

A hell of heat and drought burned across the plains of Italy. Flora and fauna, beautiful roses wilted, the olives shriveled on the bough, grapes withered on their vines. The river nymphs slowed and seeped out their life's blood into the veins of drying riverbeds. The dryads of every grove shielded their eyes from the burning sun and fled their homes, crying for the Earth Mother. She refused to hear them. She had ears for only one thing, so Ceres returned yet again to the Gods' Palaces. Jove himself came down from his throne to meet her.

"Gentle, lovely Ceres." He put an arm around her shoulders. "Have you come to a decision?"

Again, she said, "I refuse your request."

Jove sighed. "I will speak with my brother and have her released, will that appease you?"

Ceres pulled away. "Begging your pardon, My Lord, that is as it should have been, long ago! Why wait so long?"

"She's just a girl. There was never any need for you to hold her so close," he said. "Girls often leave their mothers for love."

"She did not leave!" Ceres spat. "She was stolen from me! Raped! Yet, you stand idly by and tell me she left of her own free will when you know it's not true? That does nothing to elevate you, My Lord."

She counted herself lucky when Jove shrugged off the insult. Indulging her anger wasn't normal for him. What did he have planned?

"Perhaps you will see it differently, when you have Proserpine here to explain herself."

"She will have nothing to explain. Bring her back to me, or the world will remain cold and dead." She crossed her arms. "I care not."

"That is a lie."

Ceres' face turned red with anger; she raised a hand. Jove took hold of it. "If you wish them parted," he said, "I shall see it so, if —"

"If what?"

"Pluto has a magic all his own," the mighty Jove reminded her. "If she's partaken of that then I can't fight her wishes, can I?"

Ceres narrowed her eyes. "*Her* wishes?" What were the scheming brothers up to now?

Jove sent her away with a gentle pat of his hand, and a directive, "Go and rest."

She couldn't rest and so paced her withering garden. The soil dried and cracked as she charged back and forth in her rage. She could feel it spreading out to affect the whole of Italy, the entire world.

Was it true? Would Jove finally intervene on her behalf? Or was she forever doomed to lament her child's loss?

Was he right? Fear skittered down her spine. *Did Proserpine go of her own will?* The goddess shook her head. No, that couldn't be. Her daughter would never consent to be the queen of such a vile man as Pluto; the mere idea was insane.

***

The well-tended streets of Hades sped by beneath the clomping hooves of Pluto's night-dark steeds, and Proserpine tried to take it all in. At the shores of Styx, thousands of shades lined up, waiting patiently. She could just see the wake from Charon's barge stirring the waters. He had departed not long ago.

She itched to see the Elysian Fields, the Plains of Asphodel, and Tartarus, but Pluto turned his chariot down the brighter road. Looking back, she could see the gleaming steel towers of the horrible Furies. Megaera stood over a criminal, her serpent locks hissing at him; Alecto, brandished her bloody sword at another; Tisiphone guarded the prison grounds, her bloodstained cloak pulled at a jaunty angle over her shoulder, daring any brave enough to try and stop the work she and her sisters did here. The winds couldn't quite dissipate the gut-wrenching stench of the condemned, and Proserpine put a hand to her nose.

"You will become accustomed to the sights, sounds and scents of my world," Pluto said. But Proserpine rather doubted it.

Further on, the waters of Lethe tinkled as it ran, like the sounding of a million tiny silver bells; Acheron's whirlpool of boiling mud sent steam into the sky, the slimy stench of navy Cocytus churned and poisoned the stagnant air. Hydra and monsters of all shapes and sizes loomed over the shades. Horrid screech owls and vultures dined on what, she didn't wish to know. The reek was almost too much to bear. Three Judges rested in the shade of a sagging oak, dealing with each new arrival in turn, turning each shade aside to their destination, depending on their lives' stories. The Elysian Fields glinted golden in the sunlight; laughter and deep sighs of longing love rang on the winds; the drab plains of Asphodel awaited some, Tartarus for others. She shuddered to think of with what she shared these streets.

Melos saluted Pluto as his chariot sped past.

"Not much longer now." Pluto's voice broke through the realm's din. "This road leads on towards your new home."

Excitement shivered through Proserpine and she leaned forward, squinting, yearning for a glimpse of the fabled palace.

Sitting dead center of the kingdom, the majestic golden-bricked House of Pluto rose up. The excited barks and yowls of Cerberus greeted them as they approached the elaborate gates. She knelt before the hound, and patted and rubbed its three heads, while its tongues licked her hands in delight.

The elaborate carvings on the golden doors glinted in the muted sunlight. They squeaked loudly as two hulking minotaurs pulled them wide. Inside, beauty abounded, negating everything she had glimpsed in Tartarus. Here, torches and lanterns filled the palace with warm, inviting light. Music filled the air, and statues appeared to come alive as they passed. Servants bowed and seemed to hang on their Lord's every word.

Pluto laid his warm hands to her cheeks, rested his forehead against hers. "What think you now? Do you still wish to leave?"

The thought of all she'd seen, the beauty, the sorrow. No. A scheme brewed in her thoughts as she realized she could do something here. She gave him her answer, with a kiss. "Not just yet."

A crone of a serving woman, with wiry black hair standing out every which way, gaunt face, and icy, talon-like fingers, took her hand, drew her towards the stairs, her greetings and the slap of her sandals echoing off the marble and bone walls.

Sweet scents filled the room, amber, cedar, wafting from her bath as her new serving ladies tended to her; the soft tug of combs and fingers through her hair as gems were woven into her coif, the whisper of fine linen as she donned an exquisite black tunic, over which the ladies draped a fine spider-silk stola, gray as the stormy evening sky, edged in silver and dappled with diamonds. Their chatter informed her of gossip from all the worlds. More than she'd ever heard before.

Servants gnarled with age loaded the table in the main hall end to end with succulent meats and fruits, the finest wines. Guests both lovely and alarming, human and beast, bowed to her as if she had already taken vows as their queen. Best of all, Pluto smiled, radiant as she joined him. He kissed her cheek and led her down to her seat at the head of the throng. "I see some of my minions frighten you. Don't let them."

She gulped, scanning the assembly. A quiver of fear running through her to see all eyes on her.

"What think you of my home?" Pluto asked.

"It's — "

What could she say? The look on her face must have answered for her. He patted her hand. "You'll get used to it."

She hoped so, and hoped her mother wouldn't kill her when she learned of this decision. She wondered if the quiver crawling up the base of her spine was her trepidation, or if, somehow,

Mother already knew and was having a fit even now.

***

Time slithered slowly by like a bloated adder. Usually Ceres never thought of its daily passage — welcomed it, even. Today, it was more than she could take. Would Jove be able to wrest Proserpine from his brother's control? Would she ever see her beloved daughter again?

Night fell, morning arrived, afternoon, dusk, sunset, night returned and nothing. Ceres paced worriedly. *No Proserpine, no spring. Let them die.* She would not change her mind. What was happening? *What's taking him so long?*

Finally, the knock, and Jove's voice came from her front stoop, thundering softly, as the threat of a future storm, held at bay. Ceres rushed into the foyer and thrust the door back. Jove stood proud, and strong, with a look of strange sadness on his face.

Ceres cared nothing for that, for beside him stood Proserpine — her beloved, lost Proserpine!

"Daughter!" She pulled the girl into her arms, tears blurring her vision as she hugged and covered her daughter's face in welcoming kisses.

Proserpine wept, returning her mother's embrace, and several times said something Ceres didn't quite understand, but finally, she realized.

Proserpine's kisses tasted nothing like usual; rather, Ceres thought she detected a hint of ash. "Oh, my!" She grasped her daughter's hand tightly, her own palm sweaty. It couldn't be true! "Proserpine, you didn't! You didn't accept him."

Jove sighed tiredly. "She did."

Ceres wailed and reached out for her door, her daughter, something to steady her. "She can't! She must remain with me."

Jove shook his head sadly.

Ceres growled her frustration and her willow trees groaned in answer. "I promise you, Jove, your world will end, for this!"

"No, Mama." Proserpine took her mother's hand as she pleaded, "Mama, listen. We have come to an agreement, and you must, as well."

She gave her daughter a suspicious look. "What kind of agreement?"

"I must stay with him."

Ceres gasped, and Proserpine took a step back, as if afraid.

"I may visit you from time to time," she said, "but Hades' home shall be mine as well."

Ceres gaped aghast in disbelief. "What?"

"I don't know how to choose between you, but I will, if you disagree." Proserpine bit her lip. "Please, Mama, agree. You will see he's not so bad." Proserpine sheepishly looked away and dug a toe into the floor tiles. "He's really sweet when he wants to be."

Ceres' eyes narrowed. "Is he?"

Proserpine looked up; light cheeks flushed the pink of a rose. "He proposed to me."

"Marriage?" Ceres wondered if her heart stopped. "You're to be his wife?"

Her daughter nodded, twisting her fingers as she bit her lip. "Can you believe it?"

Ceres glared at Jove, fists clenched around her daughter's arms. "Is this true?"

"I am afraid it is," the god agreed. "I promised you it would not be an easy thing to separate them. Now, will you accept them, or no?"

Ceres sighed, and gazed upon her lovely daughter, and the drought-riddled landscape, beyond.

"Mama," said Proserpine, wiggling from her hold, "it will be fine. You'll see."

"How can it be?"

"Love makes everything fine, doesn't it?"

"You love him?" The pink in the girl's cheeks deepened. Impossible! How could she love that fiend?

It couldn't be true. Ceres glared at Jove, ice frothing the stare. "What kind of trick is this?" she demanded.

"No tricks." Proserpine slipped her arm through her mother's. "Oh, Mama, wait until you hear what I have planned for them." Mischief lit in her gaze. "Think of what I could do there!"

"Do?" Could her daughter change something in the dark realm? She'd never considered any such thing before, but as she welcomed Proserpine once more into her arms, she understood perfectly.

"I will come and tell you about it, in the spring, when I return."

Ceres thought she felt her heart seize within her chest. "What do you mean? You — you have a schedule?"

The maiden goddess shrugged. "Who doesn't?"

Ceres opened her mouth to forbid this silly plot, and yet, hesitated. Maybe, after all, her daughter was right. Though she was reluctant to give that bitch Venus any credit, maybe Proserpine would be all right, perhaps even thrive as the Underworld's queen.

She looked to Jove to see him smiling behind his great white beard. Turning to her daughter, she fingered the bone pomegranate resting against her chest. *What's a few months?* She sighed, resigned. "When should we set the wedding?"

Ceres and Proserpine hugged one another once more and as they crossed the frozen landscape, Ceres lamented the cruelty of Fate. As they walked and planned the wedding, overseeing the decorations for the ceremony, as Proserpine welcomed her new husband to their hallowed, pillared temple at Enna, and fiddled with the dainty white ribbons streaming down from her crown of slim pomegranate leaves, Ceres noticed her dread lightened to see her daughter's joy.

The ice and snow melted, along with her heart; flowers bloomed in their wake, setting the sacred mount ablaze in color, and coaxed spring from her cozy bed to brighten the land.

*[This story originally appeared in the Autumn Equinox 2012 issue of **Eternal Haunted Summer**. Included here with kind permission.]*

The Unexpected Visitor: A Modern Hellenic Tale of Winter Solstice Eve

by Melia Brokaw

A servant peers upon the dinner party with trepidation. He fidgets in place as he tries to figure out the best way to interrupt his Lord and Lady, deliver his important news without letting the guests know that there is a problem in the realm. He looks over the assembly noting that tonight it is a small party, just his dark-clad lord, his lovely bride in brown and burgundy and their guest who is rather painful to look upon.

His fidgeting and hand wringing attracts the notice of his mistress. "Yes, Gerald? Is there a problem?"

The servant starts to go to her side, when her husband also speaks. "Out with it. There can be nothing here worth that level of anxiety. Have the girls been at it again?"

"There is knocking at the gate."

"Knocking at the gate?!" says the royal couple in unison.

Their brightly attired guest speaks up, "I take it that is unusual?"

The king stands up in such haste that his heavily adorned chair threatens to tip over. "Where are the hounds? Where is Kerbie?!"

"Their whimpering can be heard but no one has had the nerve to look out …"

"Very unusual," states the shining guest.

The couple, moving as one, rushes out of the room leaving their guest chuckling in glee, but too lazy to bother following his hosts. "All in time," he mutters as he swallows the liquid in his cup. "All in good time."

***

By the time the king reaches the gate, his face is dark with worry and anger. A man of few words, he gestures for the gate to be open, while his wife stands quietly at his side.

"About time someone opened up. Your hospitality is rather lacking." States a heavily cloaked woman, stooped with age.

"Mother?!" says the queen in shock. "What are you doing here?!" Rushing to her mother's side, she displays dismay at the physical state of her parent. Helping the unexpected visitor over the threshold, she looks at her husband in confusion.

"What have you done to my dogs!" thundered her husband not knowing what else to say. Internally he worried over what this visit would mean to his realm, his new marriage and politics in general.

"Ah, so he doesn't keep you locked up. I had wondered. The rumors of your willingness are proved true. How you pain me, girl." Looking at her son-in-law as she unwinds the black fabric from her upper body she states, "as for your mutts, they are fine … just a little tied up at the moment. Getting vines to grow down here was harder and yet easier than I thought it would be."

Haides groaned. "Why are you here Demeter? Why have you left the surface for this trip to Gaia's belly? Why have you deserted your realm for my own?"

Persephone stares in horror at the disheveled state of her golden mother. Her hair is white and unkempt while her skin reflected an age much older than when she last saw her mother months before. Despite her feisty demeanor, the eyes of the earth mother appear reddened and defeated.

Looking at her daughter arrayed as befitting a queen, "I was advised to come see how you fared with my own two eyes. Never did like you in dark colors. Suits you well enough, I suppose."

With that the gates are closed and servants are sent to the Harpies with requests to cut loose the hell hounds and Kerberos. "That will give the girls something to do other than harry the servants." Hades whispers to his wife as she helps her mother up the stairs.

Persephone nods and whispers, "If you will return to our guest, I will see to making Mother presentable and join you soon."

"I heard that. My hearing has not declined with the rest of me you know."

"But your temper certainly has."

"Becoming a queen has certainly made you impertinent."

"Becoming a wife and queen has given me the freedom to speak my mind." Calling to the upstairs servants, she requests water to be drawn for a bath.

***

The two ladies appear in the dining room with Demeter arrayed in dark gray clothing, white hair piled artfully upon her head. She has been quiet and thoughtful during her toiletry, observing the honor paid to her child in this realm of the dead. Upon entering, Haides rises from his seat, prodding their guest with his gaze to do the same. He then goes to his wife, kisses her on the forehead and seats her in her customary seat to his heart side. Courteously, he sits his unexpected visitor at the foot of the small table. While tradition would have it otherwise, he wanted his wife close and her mother not.

"Well, Helios," she says. "So this is where you've been spending your time of late."

The brightly coiffed guest, chuckles, saying "Well with what you've been doing to the land, there didn't seem much point of hanging around."

"Mother? What have you done?" asked Persephone with alarm.

"You were stolen from me. Your screams were heard. I wandered the land looking for you having no care for my duties."

"What about the mortals?" cried the horrified bride.

"Why did you eat of the pomegranate?" cried the mother.

"While the method of my beloved lord's marriage proposal was ill done, it is a love match. I am here of my free will. I ate of Hera's fruit because I wanted this marriage. His methodology was because of your refusal to ever see me as anything other than a child."

"You are *my* child and always will be! Why the scream if you want to be here? Why did you not tell me of your relationship?"

"I tried many times and many ways. You always refused to hear. You kept sending me off to pick flowers and "play" with my friends. Repeatedly calling me by my childhood nickname of Kore and refusing to see me as a woman grown. I love you but I could find no way to make you hear me. The scream happened when I suddenly was picked up from behind by Hades when he snuck up on me. The best flower in the meadow, he said. Laughter followed along with feelings of slight unease and daring when my love led me into his chariot and immediately back into his realm."

Hades interjected, "Yeah that little jaunt was just long enough for the girls to harry the servants into fits of terror. Yet it was well worth the trouble it caused in my realm, though I am dismayed to hear of what you have done to your own."

"Love, would you stop referring to those poor beings as girls. They serve an important function in the world. Please give them the respect they deserve."

Helios wasn't sure whose eyebrows were raised higher over Persephone's statement, Hades' or Demeter's. He quickly picked up his cup to disguise the smile on his face. No need to remind them he was present. Front row seat for the tale of the ages. Nice!

Hades cleared his throat and apologized to his beloved. "You assessment is valid and I will try to remember it." Turning back to Demeter, "now that you have seen your daughter and the high place that she holds, what will you do now? Will you still force her into attending you upon the surface for half the year?"

"Yes. She is my heart. Without her I have no desire to see to my duties. For the good of the mortal world and for the offerings that our relatives desire, she must return. However, as displeased as I am by this marriage, I will honor Hera's mandate and will not fight her return to you. Be aware that as the heart of the land falls to the underworld, so will the greenery. I will then teach mortals the methods of planting, harvesting and storage to see them through until my daughter springs again to the surface."

Hades slams his fists down on the table in anger, causing its contents to shake, rattle, and spill. All except for the cup of Helios, still held in his hand in case of the sudden need to drown his laughter. Persephone reaches over and places her hand upon her husband's tightly clenched fist.

"It is as my father said it would be. For me, I will have the best of both worlds: your love, respect and a home; as for above, the greenery and flowers which cannot grow down here. This is what Father meant when he said our marriage would not be idyllic."

"I thought he meant our strong personalities and grayness of our realm."

"No. You only hoped that."

"You are wise, my beautiful bride and well worth any price," bringing her hand to his mouth for a kiss. "Very well, but in return, I will let loose the seeds needed for your greenery and flowers. I will also let loose the shades, so that they too can visit their loved ones. A hunt will be sent out to retrieve them ... and you if necessary."

"It is done." Demeter stands and nimbly moves around the table to Helios's side. Grabbing him by the ear, she drags him to his feet. "You can have done with your smirking and gossip gathering. You have worked to do. It will be a long process to prepare the land again for plants."

Shoving him out the door, Demeter turns to say farewell to her daughter. At some point in this process, Persephone notices that her mother appears ... healthier. Her gown now has more dark green than gray to it, her hair is now a very pale yellow and her skin no longer sags like an ill fitting gown. "I cannot approve this marriage but I do hope you will be happy. I am glad that I came to see you and I hope in time your husband and I can find some mutual accord." Nodding to Haides, Demeter exits the dining room. Sounds could be heard of her harrying Helios and calling for her things.

"Well," huffed Persephone. "That went better than we thought it would." Haides pulls her into his embrace, nodding his ascent. His lips seeks her own in a private vow to enjoy every minute he has with her while she is close, only to have a mournful howl cause him to break off the kiss. Every minute that the realm will spare him that is.

September
by Dawn Corrigan

[Author's Note: I wrote *September* at a time when I was disappointing my parents by abandoning an academic career short of finishing a Ph.D. The experience made me aware of the tricky maneuvering involved in renegotiating the parent-child relationship as an adult, even when one had a happy childhood, even when one had caring, engaged parents. Maybe especially when one had those things.

I'd been reading tales from Greek and Roman mythology since childhood, and Demeter and Persephone was one of my favorites. During the interim when I knew I would be leaving the Ph.D. program but hadn't confessed this to anyone yet, I no longer had to pretend to read for my doctoral exams, and I found myself returning to the myth. This time it struck me how Demeter and Hades were the ones with all the agency in the story. Persephone's role was so passive. Initially she was abducted, and then she served as a point of negotiation in the struggle between Demeter and Hades, resulting in the changing of the seasons. She was essentially a pawn.

I wondered if Persephone would have a different account of the experience of leaving her childhood home. That was the starting point for my play.]

CHARACTERS

DEMETER A statuesque woman, Goddess of the Corn.

PERSEPHONE Daughter of Demeter and wife of Hades. Queen of the Dead.

HERMES A fleet-footed man. The Gods' Messenger.

SETTING

Late summer in Eleusis, a town on the outskirts of Athens. The time has arrived for Persephone to return to the Underworld to rejoin her husband Hades.

SCENE

BLACK. Then lights up on Persephone's bedroom in Demeter's house. Demeter is lying on the bed. There is also an open suitcase on the bed, and a trunk and several boxes scattered around the room.

PERSEPHONE

(Off stage) Mother, have you seen my sun lamp? (Demeter doesn't reply.) Still not talking? Fine, I'll look in the bathroom.

DEMETER

It's under your tennis clothes. (Persephone enters.)

PERSEPHONE

Thank you. (She moves to the bed and lifts a pile of clothes to reveal a long-necked lamp, which she packs into a box.)

DEMETER

I still don't understand why a person needs tennis clothes in the Underworld, Persephone.

PERSEPHONE

I told you, Mother, Hades and I play doubles regularly with a couple from the Elysian Fields.

DEMETER

(Not listening) And a sun lamp?

PERSEPHONE

That was a gift from Apollo. He gave it to me last year right before I went down and I'll tell you, it made all the difference in the world. Hades said I was like a different person!

DEMETER

Oh really? And what sort of person did Hades (Demeter says this name with distaste) say you'd become?

PERSEPHONE

Well, he didn't. But I think he meant I'm more like the person I am up here.

DEMETER

You mean like the person you are when you're with me! No! I won't have it! That man stole you, my only daughter, away from me, against your will and mine, and he shouldn't get to see the sunny person you are up here! I want you to be gloomy and depressed down there — then maybe he'll learn to appreciate the suffering he's caused!

PERSEPHONE

(Sitting on the edge of the bed) You don't really mean that, do you? Don't you want me to be happy?

DEMETER

Of course I want you to be happy. I want you to be happy up here, where you belong! You're my daughter--you should live in the open, near the forests and the farmers' fields. But no, I don't want you to be happy down there with him. Maybe if he sees how unhappy you are year after year, he'll give you back!

PERSEPHONE
(Laughing) That's not going to happen.

DEMETER
How do you know?

PERSEPHONE
I just know. Besides, Hades loves me.

DEMETER
Do you love him?

PERSEPHONE
Mother, Hades is my husband. I think in the last few years we've developed a partnership, learned to live and work together. And I feel like I have something to contribute down there.

DEMETER
What do you mean?

PERSEPHONE
Well, when I first arrived things were very poorly organized. The population of the Underworld had really mushroomed in the previous few years, and Hades didn't really have the procedures in place to deal with all the newcomers. During my first few seasons I was really too homesick to pay much attention, but recently Hades and I have been working

on improving things and I think I've come up with some really good suggestions.

DEMETER

Why didn't you ever tell me this before?

PERSEPHONE

How could I? I wanted to. Each year when I come home I think, this will be the year I'll start to share my life down below with Mother. But then when I arrive you start with the nasty comments about Hades and you rush to fill me in on what's happening above ground and — I just figured you didn't really want to know.

DEMETER

I never imagine you having a life down there. When you're gone I think of you as dormant — like the plants.

PERSEPHONE

(Resuming her packing) I know. But I'm not a plant. And don't you think it's better if I can find a way to be productive and, I don't know — content while I'm down there? Isn't that better for all of us?

DEMETER

It's better for him — that's what you mean. Much nicer to have a busy, happy wife — that way you can forget that you acquired her by wrongful abduction, ignoring the practices of civilized society and the wishes of her parents and the girl herself.

PERSEPHONE
Mother, you make Hades sound like such a rogue! He really isn't the way you describe him at all.

DEMETER
Isn't the way I describe him? Isn't a rogue? Persephone, he's King of the Dead!

PERSEPHONE
It's his job.

DEMETER
Well then he should get a new job!

PERSEPHONE
You know perfectly well that he can't — no more than you could yourself. Think about it: suppose someone told you the crops were no longer your business, you didn't have to bother about them anymore. You could just go your own way. Could you do that? Don't you think your connection to the plants is something beyond your control, that your attention is with them all the time even when you're doing something else? That's what makes them grow.

DEMETER
(Sulkily) Hades doesn't make anything grow.

PERSEPHONE
His work is part of the same cycle as yours, Mother — you know that.

DEMETER
I can't believe this is my last day with you —

PERSEPHONE
— Only for six months —

DEMETER
— And you've spent the entire day defending him. I'm beginning to think you like it down there.

PERSEPHONE
It isn't as bad as you think.

DEMETER
I can't believe you're saying this. Are you telling me you'd go down there to him even if you didn't have to?

PERSEPHONE
I'm saying this is my life, and I want to make the most of it.

DEMETER

I'm overwhelmed by your positive attitude.

PERSEPHONE

That's what Hades says, too. Actually, you two often sound a lot alike — especially when you talk about me. (Shyly) Hades says we light our way to Heaven with an ember stolen from Hell, and I'm his ember.

DEMETER

Which he stole from me!

PERSEPHONE

All right, Mother, I know. Look, it would be different if we could change things — I could see us having this discussion every year if there was a choice. But since nothing can change our situation — all I'm saying is, we should try to do our best with it. (Shutting the last box, and sitting on the bed again) Hades and I discussed it before I left, and we were thinking maybe this year you could come down for a visit. It's not as though you have a lot of work in winter, it's your slow time. You could come down and spend a few days — maybe even a week or two — and I could show you around, and you and Hades could get to know each other. Then you'd see he isn't really so bad, and maybe you wouldn't be so sad every year when I leave. What do you think?

DEMETER
I think in all of eternity I've never heard such a ridiculous idea! You want me, Demeter, the Goddess of the Harvest, the source of life, both yours and everything else's, to go traipsing about in the Underworld? It's preposterous! Persephone, you have completely lost your mind!

(There's a knock at the door.)

DEMETER
Who is it?

HERMES
Hermes.

DEMETER
Come in. (Hermes enters.)

HERMES
(Very respectful with Demeter, more casual with Persephone) Hello, Ma'am, how are you today?

DEMETER
I'm fine, Hermes, how are you.

HERMES
Fine, Ma'am. I'm here to fetch Persephone, if she's ready, but if I've come too soon I can always come back later —

PERSEPHONE

No, Hermes, you're right on time. Everything's ready. You just need to load these boxes over here.

HERMES

All right, I'll just start carrying them out. (He carries the boxes offstage in several trips.)

PERSEPHONE

I'm going now.

DEMETER

Just give me another minute.

PERSEPHONE

Of course. Listen, there is one more thing I've been meaning to talk to you about. I should have said something right away when I first got back, so we'd have some time to discuss it, but somehow I never got around to it. The thing is, Hades and I were thinking maybe we'd have a baby. We were thinking maybe even this year. I thought if I got pregnant soon then I could have the baby next year while I'm home with you. Then we thought — I mean, I was hoping — maybe you'd come down next winter to help out. That's another reason we were hoping you'd come visit this year — so you'd know your way around by the time the baby comes.

DEMETER
You want to have a baby with him?

PERSEPHONE
Mother! All right, just forget it. Forget I said anything. See you next year.

DEMETER
Persephone, wait. Don't go yet. It's just, this is big news — you should have told me sooner — now you're leaving and you hit me with this —

PERSEPHONE
I know. Just forget it, okay? We'll talk about it next year.

DEMETER
So I'd be a grandmother?

PERSEPHONE
Yeah. That's the thought.

DEMETER
Well. That might be fun.

PERSEPHONE
You think so?

DEMETER
Yes. Yes, I do.

PERSEPHONE
I'm so glad to hear you say that! Listen, I have to go now. But think about coming down for a visit, okay?

DEMETER
Okay, dear, I promise. Come here and give me a hug.

PERSEPHONE
(Persephone reaches down and hugs Demeter, who suddenly seems too weak to rise from the bed.) Goodbye, Mother! (Heading for the door, she turns and waves one last time. Persephone exits.)

DEMETER
Goodbye, dear. See you in the spring. (She sits and stares. Music up as lights dim.)

END.

Seasonal Affective Disorder
by Kim King

You suffocate thick grief in summer's heat,
by yanking weeds that choke tomatoes, beans
and peppers, hot and sweet. The hoe conceals
the pebbles underneath the soil you rake —
Cicadas drone a melancholy dirge.

In autumn, shadows lengthen over rows
of broken corn, while Leyland cypress tilt
in shifting light. You wield your shears at stems
of marjoram and lemon balm — the scents
enduring snips. The ocher leaves decay.

Midwinter wakes to chalky drifts that smooth
the earth's uneven tracts. Demeter's cries
escape in blurring icy sleet, then freeze.
In leather gloves you axe the apple wood
and stack the cords for warmth to sleep. Alone,

Persephone emerges with her seeds
that coax your leaden boots to trudge along,
through fields where rains assuage, abating
drought with drizzled fingers. Dead nettles bloom.

Let Winter Last For Aye!

by Rosanna E. Tufts

[Music and Lyrics Copyright ©2008 by Rosanna E. Tufts. All Rights Reserved.]

"Let Winter Last for Aye!" is the Finale of Act I from *The Passion of Persephone*, a rock opera written by Rosanna E. Tufts. She has moved the myth forward from Greek Antiquity, setting it in the Gilded Age. This allows for three fun twists on the myth: Persephone becomes a classic silent-movie-style damsel in distress who proves to have a core of steel; Hades becomes a black leather-clad Dom who rules the Underworld with an iron hand and leather whip; and Demeter and the rest of the Olympians are depicted as the class-conscious Social Register. (Zeus is dressed as Edward VII, Artemis is dressed like Annie Oakley.)

In a departure from the traditional interpretation of the story, Hades does not just jump up and carry Persephone off. He really wants her to like him, and he succeeds in fascinating her enough that she agrees to go with him. Only when she realizes where he's taking her, does she try to escape.

Captive in the Underworld, Persephone wrestles with her own confused attraction to Hades, and with the plight of the Spectres — what can she do to help them, considering she didn't inherit *any* of her famous parents' Divine power? In Act II, she discovers the answer ... after she submits to a whipping that turns unexpectedly erotic, much to the surprise of both Persephone and Hades!

But before that happens, Demeter begs Zeus to ride to Persephone's rescue. Though it breaks his heart, too, to lose his daughter, he has to refuse: He can't challenge Hades on his own turf, unless he were to get Poseidon to take sides, and that would cause a Civil War among the Gods.

Not even Hades hath fury like a woman scorned. In a "rage aria" worthy of Mozart, we see the consequences of Demeter's revenge, calling upon many disasters of history: a potato blight, an outbreak of ergot, a stock market crash, total socio-economic collapse. The human characters are dressed in Depression-era rags, recalling the Dust Bowl of the 1930s.

You can see and hear the staged version of "Let Winter Last for Aye!" as well as other videos from the show, by typing passionofpersephone into the search-box of YouTube. Sara Stewart, now singing at the Metropolitan Opera, plays Demeter; Rosanna Tufts herself portrays Clotho. Keep in touch for further developments on the progress of the rock opera, by filling in the Contact Us box at www.PassionOfPersephone.com. Get involved with the mounting and funding of the completed production at www.MythicRockTheatre.org.

ACT I, SCENE 9: EARTH

ARIA AND ENSEMBLE – DEMETER, THE THREE FATES, AND HUMANS: "LET WINTER LAST FOR AYE!" (FINALE OF ACT I)

DEMETER (seething with a combination of rage and despair)

If Zeus, the greatest High God,
A coward has become,
I'll make him rue this insult,
Until he will succumb!

Let clouds begin to gather,
All blotting out the Sun,
Let crops begin to wither,
Let harvest there be none!
Let flowers lose their beauty,
And leaves on trees turn brown —
I cannot do my duty
While my daughter is underground!

A Goddess is Immortal,
Yet *she's* as good as dead!
While Hades holds her hostage,
My Mother-Joy has fled!
No life from Earth emerges,
Death has the upper hand —

Let Earth be plagued with scourges,
And fallow lie the Land!

> The Sun grows ever fainter,
> As coldness fills the air —
> This name I give it: Winter!
> Descending everywhere!

My cold unending sorrow
All Life will come to fear,
I have no heart for growing
As long as I despair!
My vengeance has no quarter,
No prayer my heart will sway —
Because I've lost my daughter,
Let Winter last for aye!

Demeter exits, and the Three Fates enter with their yarn, yardstick, and scissors. The Humans assemble behind them, most dressed in faded farmers' clothing, others in beaten-up 1930s suits.

CLOTHO:	Look how the Threads of Life are changing!
LACHESIS:	Lines grow shorter than they used to be.
ATROPOS:	And cutting's happening far more often,
ALL 3:	A diff'rent picture on the Tapestry! We Three must put our heads

together,
>Now that the world's going all awry.
>To show the effect of this strange
new weather,
>(gleefully) Who gets to live … and who … must … die?

TENOR 1: Look at my potatoes!
>What's happening to them?
>The leaves become all blackened,
>With fungus on the stem!
BASS 1: The grain is not like usual,
>It's tiny and tough to grind —
SOPRANO 1: And the bread I'm baking with it
>Makes people lose their minds!

CHILD: I'm hungry, Mommy, feed me!
ALL CHILDREN: We're down to eating grass!
ALTO 1: If I can't give them something,
>Their bellies will fill with gas!
BASS 2: My corner of the market
>Collapsed, in record time.
TENOR 2: How far my fortune's fallen —
ALL: Buddy, can you spare a dime?

Snow begins to fall from the flies. The Humans crouch in fear, looking up, and slowly coming together from their various points around the stage, huddling.

DEMETER
ALL HUMANS AND CHILDREN

(wailing from offstage) Ahhhh ….
What are these frozen raindrops

That fall out of the sky?

There's ne'er been anything like them —

Can the Gods please tell us why?

Demeter re-enters, now dressed in autumnal colors. She comes to the front of the stage as the snow continues to fall. She does not see the Humans, nor do they see her. The Humans sing to each other in utter bewilderment.

DEMETER
HUMANS AND CHILDREN

My cold unending sorrow
This cold and strange new horror
All Life will come to fear,
Has filled our hearts with fear,
I have no heart for growing
Seems ev'rything's stopped growing,
As long as I despair!
The strong fall to despair!

My vengeance has no quarter,
The days grow ever shorter,
No prayer my heart will sway –
The sunlight's going away.
Because I've lost my daughter,
We can't feed our sons and daughters,
Let Winter last for aye!
Will Winter last for aye?

                      END OF ACT I

Homecoming

by Jennifer Lawrence

The price of your return is this:
To know it is never permanent.
Still, I run to meet you as you emerge from the
 darkness,
Cloaked first in the shadows that seem to cling to
 you,
Loving, as he can never love you,
Adoring, as the whole world adored you,
Stubborn, as I have been stubborn,
Ready to destroy everything living
To have you by my side again.
I leap to embrace you,
One with the sun
(The sun which also leaps to embrace you,
As the grass around your ankles —
Newly sprouted —
Surges to hold the bare soles of your feet)
And whirl you into my arms.
The birds break into an epiphany of joy
Flowers bloom where your shadow passes
(As if even that brief whisper of darkness
Is fruitful, where His darkness is not)
And all the world rejoices with me.
Daughter, Kore, Spring child,
I can smell the scent of pomegranate on your lips
As I fold you to my bosom,
And it — sweet as no other sweetness

(Not honey,
Not apples,
Not the light of Helios himself)
— can ever be
Is all too bitter a reminder:
In six short months, I must lose you again.
Therefore, let us go now,
Down through the meadows,
Down to the riverbank,
Down where the fertile mud cakes between our toes
And wash away that darkness that clings to you
So I can pretend — at least for a little while —
That you are only and ever mine,
And I will never have to say good-bye again.

A Rose In Winter

by Dana Wright

Demeter sighed and strummed her fingers on the laminated counter top. Business had been slow the first hour and that was never good. It meant she had time to grow maudlin in her thoughts. With Valentine's Day only a couple days away, the shop had been humming with activity. It was only this morning that they'd had a temporary reprieve. Elysian Fields was the most profitable florist in Olympia, Texas. As the Goddess of flowers and green growing things, she damned well meant to keep it that way. Besides, it helped to keep her mind off fretting about her daughter.

"All right out there. I can hear you thinking. Cut it out."

Demi snorted and rolled her eyes as her best friend and fellow Goddess, Aphrodite strolled out of the back room, her arms laden with a bouquet of lavender roses. The orders had been streaming in from the website non-stop.

"I know." Demeter pushed off the counter and smoothed her hands down her jeans. It was a nice look and a whole lot more fun than the robes they had worn since she could remember. The white tee shirt was her only concession. It was hard to give up a habit. Speaking of habits ... her eyes strayed to the calendar on the wall and her heart sank all over again. It was only February. At least here in Texas the winters weren't very long.

"Persephone is fine. Get a grip, hon." Aphrodite set the roses on the counter with a loud thunk. Shoving the vase back from the edge, she sent a barbed glare at her friend. "Look. What mother in law doesn't want to kill their daughter's husband? You have to get over it honey."

Demi nodded miserably. "I know." Tears stung the corners of her eyelids. "I just hate it."

"Well hate it later. Right now I'm up to my backside in orders and I need your help, okay?" Aphrodite's hair, normally not a strand out of place, fell in ringlets from the clip that held it back from her face. Her color was high and she had never looked lovelier. The purple top that hugged her curves was painted on like a second skin and her skinny jeans sported rhinestones in a decorative pattern on the back pockets — a veritable flame to the men who flocked around her like hopeful moths.

Demeter sucked in her breath and reached for a vase full of roses. Setting it on the counter in front of her, she plucked one out and began to pull off the thorns. At her touch, the flower withered and died, shrinking into a decayed mess of dried petals and wilting greenery.

"Demi!"

Tears began to fall in earnest from Demeter's eyes. "I ... I'm sorry." She dropped the dead flower and struggled to hold back the sobs.

"Demeter. You stop this right now." Aphrodite rounded on her, slamming a vase onto the counter so hard it sloshed water onto the floor. "You may have lost your daughter for a few months but a lot of people never get to see theirs again. Ever."

Shocked into silence, Demeter sucked in a gasp and wiped her eyes. "I don't understand."

Aphrodite smiled sadly and handed her an arrangement. "Deliver this for me, okay?" She handed Demi a tissue. "I want you to go the long way. Behind the building."

"Why?"

"You'll see." Aphrodite turned back to the mass of Valentine orders in front of her. The phones may have stopped ringing in a mild reprieve but the on-line orders were still going strong. "Now hurry. Thanks for helping me out with this one."

Demeter nodded, thankful for the chance to get some air and clear her head. "Sorry. I hate when I get like this."

"You and me both. Now go. Take a walk and deliver some cheer." Aphrodite slid her a look. "Just do me a favor."

"What?" Demeter shrugged into her jacket and grabbed her purse. Picking up the arrangement of cheerful daisies and bright greenery, she moved toward the door.

"Don't touch the flowers until you're out of your mood, okay?"

Demeter smiled and rolled her eyes. "Yes, boss."

"Good. Now hurry. I need you back here to help with the afternoon rush." Aphrodite jammed a lily into a funeral arrangement and waved her off.

***

The address on the card was just a few buildings over. Demeter held her face up to the sun and let the fresh air calm her. Nature always did that, even in the winter months. It was she that set the pace of the seasons, after all. Even here in this little town in Texas, she still held sway over the ebb and flow of crops and plant life. The Texas winter was a mild one and for that she was grateful. Not one to care for snow, she preferred a milder climate. Cool crisp air tickled her nose and put a spring to her step. Her boots clicked along the sidewalk as she arrived at her destination. Scanning the card to be certain, her eyes trained on the building — The Children's Hospital. Oh no.

"Sneaky girl." She muttered as she went around the building and approached the back of the hospital. For some reason Aphrodite wanted her to come in from the back. Maybe the room was close to the rear entrance. Shrugging, she made her way down the walk and found herself in front of a large circular garden. It, like everything else, was suffering from the winter season. The plant life had withered and died, making what should have been a lush display of foliage into a mass of dead greenery surrounding a large skeletonized tree.

"Now that is just depressing." Demeter sighed.

"It really is."

"Who?" Demeter whirled, searching the garden.

"Here." A young girl in a wheelchair sat off to one side, her body obscured by the trunk of the tree.

"Oh. Hello." Demeter smiled, making her way over. "I'm here looking for Charlie Sussman. He has a delivery." She held up the vase of daisies, careful not to touch them.

The girl smiled, her pale face illuminated by the rays of the winter sun. "I'm Charlie." Wrapped in the blanket, she didn't look much older than twelve or thirteen. She lifted her hands from beneath the blanket accepting the flowers. "Thanks."

"You're very welcome."

"I wish they didn't have to die."

"What?"

"The flowers. It makes me sad."

Demeter frowned. "I know. It makes me sad, too." She ran her hand along the stone of the small retaining wall.

"They should be able to be green all year round."

"Oh. You mean the plants." Demeter smiled, staring at the dead garden.

"Yes. I probably won't be around to see it next spring, so I sit out here and try to remember how it looked before."

Demeter smiled. "Well hopefully you have a nice garden at home to tend when the weather warms up."

"No, ma'am." Charlie shook her head. "I have cancer. The doctors have tried everything. Nothing seems to work." She smiled wanly.

"Oh." Demeter felt the sting of tears pulling at her eyes once more. Cancer was the worst thing in the world. "How long have you been here?"

"Six months. My dad — he sent the flowers — he had to go away on business. He'll be back on Saturday."

"That's good."

"Do you have a daughter?"

Demeter smiled, surprised. "Yes I do. She's away right now."

"That sucks."

Laughing at the deadpan tone, Demeter smiled. "Yes, Charlie. It does suck."

"I have an idea."

"What?" Charlie rolled her chair closer to where Demeter stood.

"How about we bring some life into these plants. It will be our secret garden? What do you think?"

Charlie grinned. "Now how are you going to do that?"

"Oh ... I have my ways." Demeter said evasively. "But here's the thing." She paused. "I need you to touch this leaf for me. Give it all your love. Can you do it?"

Frowning, Charlie nodded. "Okay."

"Good. Now roll a little closer." Demeter helped to push her close to the stone barrier fence surrounding the garden. "Okay. Hold on."

Fingers tingling, Demeter summoned her Goddess energies. Thinking of her daughter and the joy she would have seeing her again in just a few short months, she poured her love into the small garden and the pale shell of a girl that sat shivering in the winter chill.

Mother. I hear you.

There. Persephone was near. Did she feel the pull of the child?

Letting her thoughts reach out to her daughter, Demeter sighed. She sent her images of the girl, the garden, and the future of what would be.

I will make a place for her at my table, Mother. Hades will love her as his own.

Love for her daughter and her generous heart sent a tear sliding down her cheek. Where it fell into the earth, a tender green shoot began to grow.

"Who are you?" Charlie whispered.

"A friend." Demeter took a deep breath as the tingling became a rush of warmth throughout her body. Roses bloomed in a garden of vibrant greens and magnificent color. The skeleton tree burst forth in a frenzy of budding leaves. It was as it was meant to be. She was a Goddess. Being mired in her own sorrow, she had forgotten. There were more daughters to love than just her own. Wiping her tears, she hugged Charlie and watched the flowers as they awakened from winter's brief kiss.

"What do you say we get some hot cocoa from the cafeteria?"

"Only if they have marshmallows."

"I wouldn't have it any other way." Demeter laughed and they made their way inside, a butterfly fluttering in the warm spring breeze.

<u>Letting Go</u>
by Gerri Leen

Demeter felt the chill from the underworld come over her as she stood outside the cave that led to Hades realm. Shadows seemed to reach out, and a dark dread grew inside her as she watched Persephone stroll in the sunshine through the bare fields. In the past, her daughter would have danced, would have been singing in joy at being reunited with her mother. But now, she walked slowly, her lovely voice silenced.

"What have you done, Hades?"

He moved as close as the shadows would let him, and she felt the gripping cold of non-life. "I have done nothing. Time — time has wrought this."

Demeter moved away from him, just enough to make the cold stop, not enough to give him any more power over her life than he had by holding her daughter hostage for three months a year. She turned her eyes back to Persephone, whose manner may have changed, but her effect was still the same. Green shoots sprang forth as Persephone walked; trees breathed a sigh of relief as their lifeblood moved freely again. Soon there would be flowers in this field — Spring had returned; the mother-daughter reunion was complete.

So, why did it feel incomplete this time?

She heard a low sigh and glanced at Hades, still standing in the cave entrance when he should have left immediately after delivering her daughter to her. It was what he had always done in the past.

But her daughter had never kissed him goodbye in the past, either. Demeter closed her eyes, but the memory replayed anyway. Persephone stepping up to Hades — he had not grabbed her, had not yanked her to him and forced his kiss on her. It had not been a quick kiss, either, but a kiss of lovers, of a fully realized woman saying goodbye to the man whose bed she shared.

The kiss had been Persephone's choice. She had come back this time with her innocence tarnished, had not drunk from Lethe's forgetting waters so that she would not have to relive her three months in the underworld. Why had she chosen to not drink?

Hades was watching her daughter with a look of such longing Demeter wanted to strike him. Then Persephone turned and gazed back at Hades with the same look.

Demeter felt as if she had been struck. "She loves you?"

"So it would appear." He turned to look at her. "This disturbs you?"

"It repulses me." She felt her stomach clench at the thought of Persephone happy in her brother's dark and bitter realm.

"She is not you, and for that I am fortunate."

"Up here, on the surface, with her maidens and flowers and sunshine, she will have her life —

her true life — back, and then we shall see if she is eager to return to your damp and frigid shade."

"You have spent so little time in my realm, sister. What do you know of it?"

"I know she deserves better." She could feel the old anger, the rage and despair that had turned the fields sere and barren when she had wandered the world looking for her lost child. "You stole her from me."

"I could take her body, but her heart is hers alone to control." He moved closer, and Demeter repressed a shudder. He was her brother; they had sprung from the same womb, had lived in Cronos's gut with the others until Zeus had rescued them. But Hades disturbed her, was everything she was not. Death to her life. Gray to her brilliance. Emptiness to her plenty.

She tried to pull sunshine and warmth around her, tried to project it back on him, to make him fall away, back into his shadows and endless night. "She will not return happily."

"That remains to be seen." He smiled. A sad smile, half wistful, as if he hoped what he'd said was the truth. For a fleeting moment, Demeter almost felt sorry for him.

Then he turned and walked back to his kingdom.

Demeter walked away from the mouth of the cave and hurried out to where her daughter waited.

Small birds made crazy circles as if celebrating the return of the Maiden.

"They love you," Demeter whispered.

"And I love them."

Demeter did not mean her sigh of relief to escape with such force.

Persephone turned to stare, her eyes harsh and glittering like coal — a mineral of Hades' realm. "I love him, too."

"Yes. I guessed that was the case." She touched her daughter's hair, noticed that the light brown strands had turned darker, nearly black. She had thought it was only a trick of the shadows at the cave entrance.

Persephone leaned into her hand. "I have missed you."

"Have you?"

Her daughter gave her a sweet smile — the first since coming out of the darkness with the God of the Dead. "Of course I missed you. How could I not?"

Demeter smiled in relief. "What would you like to do first, now that you're back?"

In the past, Persephone had chosen to lounge in the foothills of Olympus, letting Demeter braid her hair and tell her all the gossip she'd missed. Or to play in the sea with Poseidon's dolphins as seabirds wheeled overhead singing a paean to her return. Or to run with her maidens, coaxing flowers from the ground by the power of her smile, the tinkling bell of her laugh.

"There are so many places I have never been," Persephone said, drawing Demeter close to her, arms linked — the way equals walked. A way they had never walked.

"You have been to all the beautiful places," Demeter murmured, trying to free her arm, to wrap it around her daughter's shoulder and pull her close. Persephone should nestle. She should be protected.

Her daughter resisted. Her grip was as relentless as death itself. "I would like to visit some of the other places."

"Other places?"

"The ones you've kept from me. The ugly places." Her smile was the sweet smile of years before. Her eyes, though, gleamed like black diamonds under the veil of newly dark hair. "You have sheltered me."

Demeter studied her daughter, tried to find the sweet, innocent maiden in the woman who stood before her, dark eyes glittering. "I did what any mother would do."

"I know it was for my own good. But it ends now." Persephone looked up, attention diverted by the call of a crow — a bird she would never have noticed in the past.

"Where do you want to go?"

"I would like to visit a battlefield of my cousin Ares — he brings so many to our realm."

Demeter swallowed hard.

"I would like to see Hecate's world of sand and dust, of snakes and scorpions. And Eris — I should like to make the acquaintance of the goddess of discord."

Demeter felt something inside her dying.

Her daughter — the goddess of life springing forth — must have realized that. She pulled Demeter to her, hugging her fiercely and laying kisses on her neck. "I love you. More than you will ever know." She let go of her. "But you have to allow me to be who I will be. I'm not your little girl anymore."

Demeter thought she could hear Hades' cold laughter. Then she realized it was Persephone, laughing at something only she could see in the far distance.

"There is so much to learn, Mother."

And then she was gone. Running away, a streak of green marking her passage as she headed to the dustbowl that was Hecate's realm.

Demeter took a deep breath. Her daughter was home.

Her daughter who she no longer knew.

For a moment, she mourned the old Persephone, the maiden who'd drunk happily of Lethe's brew, who'd wanted nothing but to forget her life as Queen of the Underworld.

Then Demeter let that Persephone go.

Following the path of green, she set out to get to know this new woman her daughter had become.

END

Pomegranate Cupcake
by Erzabet Bishop

"Get that thing out of my sight." Demeter snarled, knocking the pomegranate out of Aphrodite's hand and onto the floor with a thud. It rolled down the dais landing at the bottom of the steps.

"Wow. That wasn't bitchy at all." Aphrodite narrowed her eyes and scooped the fruit off the marble floor of the palace. These days Olympus was all but deserted. The Gods hung out in smaller places now-anywhere where their presence was revered. Greek restaurants. Movie theaters. Even a florist shop in a small town in Texas. It was disheartening to say the least.

"Look. I know you're worried about Persephone but you want to hear this."

Demeter leveled her gaze on her friend and sister Goddess. "Go on." All she wanted to do was be left in peace. Three months without her daughter by her side and it was torture. Especially when she thought about the handsome dark haired God Hades. He tricked Persephone and now she was married to him-destined to spend three months out of the year at his beck and call. It was mortifying that a daughter of hers would succumb to his wiles and go willingly to the Underworld. Hadn't she taught her better than to wander close to Hell's portals? Demeter closed her eyes and clenched her teeth. Her friend meant well, but talking about the situation just made it worse. For more years than she cared to think about, she let all of nature wither and die as she mourned the loss of her daughter's innocence, suffering her absence in the winter months. When Persephone was with her, all was right. Even if she had to endure Hades insufferable presence at the dinner table. He was a domineering oaf and she hated the way Persephone followed his every command.

"Hades is giving one of his infamous parties at the Elysian Club tonight. I hear tell that Persephone is going. Do you want to sneak in and see if you can talk to her?"

Demeter sighed. "He'll see me and I would never live it down."

Aphrodite shook her blond curls, her lips curving up in a devious smile. "Nope. Not a chance. It's a masked affair, so all the party-goers will be anonymous."

"What?"

"Yep. And I have the perfect costume for you."

"You've lost your mind."

Aphrodite snorted. "Are you afraid?"

"I really don't want to see my daughter in a place like the Elysian Club." Demeter crossed her arms under her breasts, her lips pressing into a thin line. She knew her daughter was an adult, but still. It didn't have to be rubbed in her nose.

"It's a club. What people do behind closed doors is their business. But you can see her on the main party floor to be sure she's okay. She'll never know you were there."

Demeter played with the folds of her robe. "But what would I wear?"

Aphrodite grinned. "Oh ... you leave that to me. Goddess of Love, remember?"

"How could I ever forget?" Demeter rolled her eyes. It was going to be a long night.

***

"What were you thinking?" Demeter hissed. Her eyes blazed as they looked down her body. Tight leather bustier, flouncy micro skirt that barely covered her backside, thigh high boots and an up do that made her head want to loll from her neck. A lacy mask covered half of her face.

"I was thinking we could finally have a good time instead of you sulking like a child." Aphrodite sniffed, pushing her forward in line. The graceful lines of her almost transparent lavender gown made Demeter blush behind the mask. Aphrodite didn't look like herself at all. Short cropped red hair and a fluttery butterfly mask made her look like a naiad.

The Underworld was hopping and the traffic in front of the club was horrendous. The line to get inside was long, but moved quickly. Cerberus acted as bouncer, a pomegranate the price of admission.

"How droll." Demeter hated the cursed fruit that secured her daughter's fate. Three seeds and her life had changed forever. Persephone was bound to grow up, but she would have like it if it were a little more on her terms.

"Quiet. You want him to figure out it's you?" Aphrodite growled, elbowing her friend in the side.

"Ouch!" Demeter started, sucking in her breath. Her feet wobbled in the boots and she stumbled into the arms of the man behind her in line.

"Oh!"

"Had a little too much to drink there cupcake? You only just got here."

Demeter spun around, her lips already twisting in a retort. Her eyes settled on the muscular form of the man in front of her and her mouth went dry. Broad shoulders and sculpted abs filled out the skin tight black tee shirt. Leather pants fit along muscular thighs and long legs sliding into biker boots. A delicious warmth settled in her stomach and a tingling settled over her body. He was Adonis personified.

"Well hello there." Aphrodite maneuvered herself between Demeter and the handsome stranger.

"Hello yourself." Mr. Handsome's lips quirked up flirtatiously.

Demeter rolled her eyes. The spark she felt when she first took in his bad boy withered and winked out. Why would anyone possibly look at her twice with the Goddess of Love standing next to her? Even in these borrowed clothes, she still felt like herself and a coquettish nymph she was not.

Snorting, Demi moved forward, leaving Aphrodite to her conquest. She would go in, have a look around just long enough to make sure Persephone was okay and that would be that.

"Where are you going, cupcake? Afraid I might bite?"

Demeter stopped in her tracks. Spinning on her heel, she found herself staring into the tight tee shirt of Mr. Handsome. Aphrodite stood a few steps behind, hands on her lips and a bemused expression on her face.

"Go on!" Aphrodite half whispered, waving as she found another candidate for her amorous affections a few feet down in line.

Demeter rolled her eyes. Lifting her chin, she met the challenge in Mr. Handsome's gaze. How had she not noticed the piercing gray color of his eyes before?

"My name is not Cupcake."

"Really? And here I thought you were one of those brainless Goth chicks Hades usually invites to his raves."

"I can assure you, if that's what you're looking for, you have the wrong woman."

"Oh ... I think I've found just what I'm looking for." Jauntily he cocked his head to one side.

His eyes burned into her and Demeter felt her knees grow weak. Her lips parted in response to his suggestive comment, but before she could say a word, he pulled her into his arms and sealed his lips to hers.

Shoving him away, Demeter growled. "I ought to teach you some manners pretty boy."

A spark lit in the stranger's eyes. "Oh, lady. Now that would be the icing on the cake."

"That's it." Demeter promptly disengaged herself from his grip. Giving him a curt nod of farewell, she hurried to catch up the line. Bastard. Who the blazes did he think he was? Before she knew it, she was through the door and in the club. Aphrodite was nowhere to be found. What she did see made her eyes almost roll back in her head. Men, women and shades strolled about in a semi-dressed state. Women danced in cages as the lights flickered and strobed. The scent of brimstone and too many bodies, both living and dead assaulted her nostrils. The crowd moved and pulsed to the tech-no-pop music that vibrated through the room. It was electrifying. It was too much.

Staggering to the wall, Demeter sighed. How would she ever find her daughter here? Would she even want to? Wobbling on the too high boots, she straightened herself. A shade floated by, offering her pomegranate seeds.

"No thank you." She said through tight lips. She was not some foolish mortal willing to be trapped in the Underworld. At the thought, she flinched. Persephone. She needed to see her for just a moment and she could give up this ridiculous charade. She was not a twenty something human with a death wish and a micro skirt. The shade nodded and moved away, his task to claim as many unsuspecting playmates for his master. The slime.

A parade of leather clad party-goers danced through the center of the room. At the tag end of the proceedings was none other than her Persephone. Rigged from head to toe in a tight leather corset and form fitting leather pants that blended into magnificently high boots, she wielded a whip at the unfortunate man in front of her.

The music paused long enough for Demeter to hear the whip connect with the man's flesh and his agonized wail. The leather mini brief he wore was barely decent and a fine red line appeared on his back.

"What do we say Hades? I don't think I heard you right?" Persephone arched one finely shaped eyebrow and tilted her blood red lips into a sensual frown.

"Yes, Mistress. I'm sorry Mistress. You won the wager."

"I thought so. Tomorrow is another day, but tonight you wear my collar." She bent down and fastened a black leather collar around the King of the Underworld's neck. Re-securing the leash, she gave it a firm tug.

"Well I'll be damned." Demeter stared with wide eyes. Her daughter had things better in hand than she realized.

"Yes. You'd have to be to be here Cupcake."

Demeter sighed and tore her eyes away from the couple. "My name isn't Cupcake."

"I never thought it was."

"Want to get a coffee?"

"Oh Gods, yes." Demeter looked out over the leather clad people and shook her head. It was hard to go from a white toga to a micro skirt in one night. She paused, eyes searching for her daughter and Aphrodite once more. No. They had their own lives to lead. Maybe it was time for her to do the same.

"Let's go." Mr. Handsome held out his hand, eyes twinkling in the strobes and light show. "Do you need to wait for your friend?" He frowned, noting her hesitation.

Demeter stopped, her gaze meeting his. She held out her hand. "No. My name is Demi. Nice to meet you."

He laughed, pulling her away from the wall. "Nick. Come on. It only gets rowdier the later it gets."

"I'll bet." Demeter brushed a bit of Underworld off her skirt. "Let's go."

"Come on. I know this great little town you might like in Texas. Has a coffee shop that serves some great lattes."

A smile curved Demeter's lips. "I can hardly wait." They strolled through the door and out into the night air. The line for entrance into the club had grown since they were inside.

"There's also a rumor they have killer cupcakes," Nick murmured and winked.

"Not nice." Demi swatted him in the arm, grinning.

"You have no idea." Nick's eyes blazed bright with promise.

The weight of worry faded away. Finally. Persephone would be alright. As she stepped in the dead grass, flowers bloomed. "Life, love and cupcakes." She snorted as a particularly persistent night blooming flower brushed her ankle in thanks. It was time for her now. A pomegranate lay abandoned in the grass and she considered it for the briefest of moments. Her foot swung forward in a kick, the vicious boots sending it careening into the darkness beyond.

"Come on. I have an idea what you can do with some triple chocolate frosting." Demi looped her arm in his as they wandered into the mists.

Through the Pain
by Jen McConnel

When she vanished,
You wept salt tears.
The earth could not conceal
your daughter from You,
and yet, for a time,
You were lost.
Like a mortal.

You remind us that pain
can cripple
even the strong,
and You show us
that sometimes, solitude
is best.

These are not the only lessons
You teach:

From You, we learn to rise anew
from the tears and face the dawn.
Because of You, we know
that spring will come again.

Erysichthon
by Kate Taylor

It was first light on a winter's morning and Owen was already at work. Around him fallen trees lay like casualties of a war, their bare branches bleached bone white by the frost. Owen tried to keep his eyes on the faint sunrise staining the horizon but instead he found himself picking out the trees he'd helped fell.

The protesters had left after the last tree was cut down, looking broken and defeated in their VW vans, their hybrids, their family cars, their rainbow scarves and trailing sleeves, their thermals and winter coats. Some of them had been crying and Owen had put down his chainsaw as they filed past: a small sad funeral procession.

Now Owen stamped across the frozen ground in an attempt to avoid chilblains. A noise snapped him out of his thoughts. Somewhere nearby someone was crying. It was not the abandoned crying of a child but grown up tears, punctuated with odd gasps and bitten off wails. It was coming from behind one of the fallen trees and for a moment it sounded as though the tree itself was crying.

There was a woman sitting on the icy ground. Her hair was the colour of summer wheat and it fell across her shoulders like a cloak. One hand rested lightly on the tree's trunk, as though she was comforting a sick child. She must have been freezing.

Her dress was modest enough, falling to her feet but her arms and most of her shoulders were bare. No coat, no thermals he could see, just flimsy green fabric. Her feet were bare too, unless you counted the smattering of frozen mud. Owen had seen women wearing less in the depths of winter but only on nights out and never barefoot.

'Jesus Christ,' Owen said, tearing off his fluorescent vest so he could offer her his coat. 'You'll get frostbite.'

The woman only glared and got to her feet without his help. She ignored his jacket.

'Did you do this?' she said, throwing an arm out wide to encompass the fallen wood. Sometimes Owen could barely move from cold by the last hours of his shift but the woman didn't even wince. If it hurt her to stand on the frozen ground she showed no sign of it. 'It's carnage.'

Owen felt his hackles rise: he'd had a lot of that lately, off the neighbours, off people he'd barely said three words to, even Chloe didn't like where his wages were coming from, although she said she understood.

'What do you expect from a building site?' he demanded. 'They're going to build it with or without me. Only this way I get to put food on the table.'

'And that's enough, is it?' The woman asked. Owen had had protesters scream and rail and throw clods of frozen earth at him. It was nothing to the look in the woman's eyes. 'And what about the farmer? How will he eat?'

'Look, he was paid. The lease was up: it's not like they stole the site off him,' Owen said, with all the conviction that he could manage. It was a source of local bitterness. The family hadn't wanted to leave but they couldn't win a bidding war, even with the loans, the money borrowed from friends, even (or so Owen heard) after selling the family silver. There was talk of a boycott but Owen doubted it would stick: not once people got used to having a supermarket so close.

Instead of standing in the cold arguing he put his coat around the woman's shoulders and marched her inside, ignoring her protests. The metal portacabin was like stepping from a fridge into a deep freezer but Owen pushed the woman into a seat and switched on the heater. There'd be trouble later: he wasn't supposed to switch it on until the first team arrived but he was damned if he was having anyone catch hypothermia on his watch.

'Do you take milk?' he asked, filling the kettle and switching it on. 'Tea or coffee?'

The woman didn't answer. She was watching him with a kind of detached curiosity as though she wanted to see what he'd do next.

Owen put a tea bag in each mug, added water, stirred milk into his.

'It's too late you know,' he said more gently, putting a mug down in front of her and sitting down himself. 'The trees are gone.'

'They weren't ordinary trees,' she said. 'There was a shrine here in Roman times. People would travel for days, sometimes for weeks, to pray for fertility and a good harvest. They called her Ceres.'

She hadn't touched her tea.

'I didn't put milk in,' he prompted. 'In case you were vegan or something.'

'Vegan?'

'My wife's a vegetarian,' Owen continued. 'Ever since the horse meat scandal she won't eat the cheap stuff and we can't afford organic.'

'Do you know why the Brits won't eat horse meat?'

'Horses are expensive to keep.'

'No more expensive than in France. The Anglo-Saxons used to ritually slaughter and eat horses: something to do with absorbing their power. Of course the church stamped it out. And we're still feeling the effects today.'

'So you are what you eat? Don't think Chloe'd appreciate it if I called her dolphin-safe tuna. Or a vegetable. She wasn't keen on meat before mind: all those animals raised in the dark and fed on steroids.'

The woman looked pained. 'It's not right. But more people are born everyday and the world gets smaller ....' She raked one hand through her golden hair. 'I don't know what the answer is.'

She sounded tired. Not the slurred voice and bad coordination of someone who'd been up all night sabotaging diggers and chaining themselves to trees. This was the bone deep weariness of someone who spent every day fighting just to stand still.

She was starting to shiver as she warmed up, the way people did after they'd been really cold. Owen took off his gloves and handed them to her.

'You're being very kind to me,' she said. 'Why?'

Owen shrugged. 'You can't just leave people barefoot in the snow.'

'It's not snowing.'

'Frost then. It's only what I'd want someone else to do if they saw Chloe out in this weather.'

'Is Chloe your wife?'

'My pregnant wife.' Owen smiled mirthlessly. 'It's amazing what you're prepared to betray when you've got kids to feed.'

'How many do you have?'

'Two little girls and a third on the way,' Owen said, smiling properly this time.

'I had a daughter once. She'll be visiting soon.'

'Lives with her dad, does she?' Owen asked, hoping that this would be less awkward than saying nothing.

'Her husband,' the woman frowned. 'You wouldn't believe the trouble I had with him. Took it into his head that they were made for each other when she was still a slip of a girl and then there was no stopping him. I'd visit but I can't be around him. Physically can't.'

'He a bad sort or something?' Owen asked stirring more sugar into his tea. She didn't look old enough to have a married daughter.

'Oh he'd never hurt her and he's never cheated,' the woman said. 'But he took her away from me and I can't forgive that.'

'Don't know what I'll do when mine take up with boys,' Owen said.

'You won't stop it,' the woman said, staring into her mug.

She looked as though she was about to cry again and without thinking about it, Owen reached over and squeezed her hand.

'I used to hate him you know,' she said tonelessly. 'She could have been anything and now she's stuck with him. But now I see her and she's happy and I wonder if I was forcing her to be something else too.'

'You did the best you could,' Owen told her. 'There's nothing wrong with wanting the best for your kids.'

She gripped his hand and made an odd choking sound, smiling despite herself. She was beautiful, Owen noticed, almost unnaturally so. He wondered how he'd missed it.

'I suppose I should be glad she's happy down there,' the woman said.

'Southerner is he?'

The woman laughed. 'About as southern as they get.'

'Well there's nothing wrong with that,' Owen said. 'Every where's south of somewhere.'

'You've been kind to me,' the woman said, getting to her feet and smoothing of her skirt 'Don't come into work tomorrow. Take your family and leave. This town is dying.'

'It's the recession,' Owen answered. 'Things are tight everywhere.'

'No. This town is marked for death.' She opened the door. Outside the mist had lifted - the site looked like an open wound.

Owen felt a sudden chill, right down to his bones. It was the cold air getting in, he told himself. The door was open. That was all.

'Oh?'

'Once I'd have cursed its crops to failure and sent disease to plague its livestock. But a supermarket kind of defeats the point,' she smiled bitterly. 'And they said the Greeks were the only ones who could do irony.'

'What then?' Owen was familiar with pagans. Chloe had been one in her youth, although he'd understood that most frowned on curses.

'I have a brother,' the woman said, making her way down the metal steps. If the freezing metal hurt her feet she showed no sign. 'Doesn't like our family being insulted.'

'If you wait until someone gets here I can talk the foreman into letting me give you a lift,' Owen said. 'You shouldn't be walking around like that.'

'Don't worry about me,' the woman said, standing on tiptoe to kiss him on the cheek. 'Go with my blessing, Owen. And remember, don't come into work tomorrow.'

***

Owen was too distracted to notice if anyone looked at him strangely for the rest of his shift, although Chloe was quick enough to point it out when he got home.

'There's a mark on your cheek,' she told him.

Owen ducked into the hall to see for himself in the mirror. There was a poppy coloured smear on his jaw, the same shape as the strange woman's kiss.

'You should be ashamed, coming home to your pregnant wife with another woman's lipstick all over your face,' Chloe called after him. She was teasing but wouldn't be if he didn't volunteer an explanation.

'Come here,' Chloe said, scrubbing at it with her sleeve after he'd explained everything as far as he understood it. She only succeeded in turning his whole cheek red with irritation and when it faded the mark was still there, smeared into the shape of a poppy. 'You must be allergic.'

'She didn't even look like she was wearing makeup,' Owen muttered.

'Stop staring at other women's mouths.' Chloe stuck her tongue out at him. 'Look, don't worry about curses: only the gods can curse people.'

It started to sleet as they went to bed, a soft insistent patter which kept him awake late into the night. Only when the wind started up, howling through the power lines and tearing at the trees did he fall into a restless sleep.

In Owen's dreams the cranes and diggers were gorging themselves on the dark earth, tearing through ligaments, spitting out stones like fragments of bone. Down and down they went, until the forest was a cavern. There were people down there, Owen realised. The dream got markedly worse after that.

It was jumbled, if jumbled was the right word for something with sharp edges and hidden drops. The air around him seethed, white, then blue-black, then white. There was a roaring all around him so deep he felt it as much as he heard it. There were other noises too: screams and the sound of metal buckling.

He woke in a still-dark bedroom to the touch of a woman's hand on his forehead.

'Go to sleep, Owen,' she said, in a voice as soft and cool as her palm.

'Sorry, Chlo,' he muttered. 'Nightmare.'

'What's that?' Chloe called from the bathroom.

Something suddenly seemed deeply wrong but his limbs, his eyelids, even his thoughts were heavy. Sleep closed over him like a fist.

By the time he woke up the sky was beginning to turn light and his shift was half over. He yanked his clothes on so hard he almost tripped, swearing under his breath so as not to wake Chloe. There was no time for breakfast but he grabbed an apple on the way out the door, knowing he wouldn't get chance to eat it.

***

He saw the lights before he even reached the turning. Ambulances were streaming away from the site. The sirens weren't blaring but that only made them seem worse, the way doctors got all quiet when they were delivering bad news. As he reached the site he saw a fire engine levering one of the cranes upright and firemen digging into the twisted metal underneath. There were police cars too and the red-white builder's tape had been replaced with yellow-black.

'I'm supposed to be starting my shift,' he told a policeman, surprised at how detached his own voice sounded.

'Not much chance of that now,' the man replied, his face grim. 'You want to go home. Count your blessings you didn't have the early shift.'

'What happened?' Owen asked.

'Lightning,' the policeman said, taking his helmet off as the last of the ambulances made its way down the lane. 'Apparently one of the cranes wasn't grounded properly. Everyone was sheltering in the portacabin with the weather like it was.' He shook his head. 'Go home. I wouldn't be here if I didn't have to be.'

There were human corpses now, laid out among the fallen trees. The red blankets covering them were stark against the white ground: from a distance it looked as though the trees were bleeding. Owen shivered and turned away.

*[Originally published in the Winter Solstice 2013 issue of **Eternal Haunted Summer**. Included here with kind permission.]*

Demeter Melaina

by P. Sufenas Virius Lupus

The dark mother, earthen-black
was wronged by the sea-god,
ravished in her Arcadian temple.

But she did not yield in defeat
nor lose her ferocity amidst
the assault on her sovereignty.

Earth, though smaller, is greater
than the wide expanse of sea,
ever-higher, ever-deeper it lies.

Poseidon had not been "earth-shaker"
before he had raped Demeter;
nor was he after the incident ...

... For it is the Mother, ever-angry
at his encroachment upon her
that shakes in rage and resentment.

The offspring of his sacrilege,
Areion the horse of wonder
was the foremost child of Arcadia.

And Black Demeter, furious
wreaks her vengeance across time
for the injustice done to her.

For Demeter

by Jennifer Lawrence

I kneel in the oven of the sunlight,
Beating down on my back like a whip.
My hands would never win any beauty pageants —
Nails broken and caked with rich soil,
They sneeringly proclaim my low interests.
I dig deep, nesting the seedling into the hole I've created,
Then pack the dirt around it, gentle as a lover.
There aren't many weeds this early in the season;
Nonetheless, I pinch and I pluck, nagging at the
Little green things growing where they don't belong.
All around me, I can see tiny emerald shoots starting to
Peep up out of the soil:
Onions, corn, garlic and tomatoes,
Broccoli, radishes, beets, peppers.
There are flowers on the raspberry vines and the strawberries.
At an age and circumstance beyond bringing forth children from my womb,
Still I create life.
Sweat trickles into my eyes and I wipe it away absently,
Not realizing until hours later that there's a black streak smeared
Across my brow.

There is nothing in my mind but
Soil
Seeds
Water,
And although sometimes I don't know it,
With every breath I sing your name.

Dem & I

by C.D. Coss

The starter wheel didn't turn despite the kicks from Dem's horseshoed boot-heel. He wrapped his hand around one of the tractor's turf studded steel wheels and balanced for a bigger blow.

" — piece of shit," he cursed it. "I could pull the plow my own damn self for all the time I spend fixing this thing."

"Get down, 'Dem, you're only going to wear out your shoes kickin' on it."

"It's almost moved, if I can just get one good one at it — "

He reared his boot till the leg-seam of his overalls was perpendicular with the ground, bringing his movement down with a fury that bounced off and left him grasping at the sheening green sheet metal as be fell back onto the dusty barnyard.

"Goddamn thing!" he shrieked with a cracking voice as I stifled a laugh.

He charged up to the farmhouse, read-faced and swearing and stomping.

"Ask Demeter how long 'til suppers on!" I shouted after my brother.

"And make sure Mama kisses up your boo-boo real nice," I mumbled, as I pushed my pressed shirtsleeves up and pulled myself onto the tractor with the hand that wasn't holding the axle grease.

***

" — you still got to watch, just a little rain messes things all sorts of ways," I said across the table to 'Dem, trying to explain the seized engine as I passed the china-plate heaped with greens to Pa and took the pickled ham from Demeter, our Ma.

"That'd be a hell of a luck, too," Pa grunted in reply, clanking a spoon of greens down, "ain't had rain for going on three weeks."

"It's true," 'Dem agreed, his tanned wrinkled forehead hiding the long bruise from his go with the starter wheel.

I hadn't washed my own face coming in, trying to add some color to my pallid hue, and I'd left my jacket on the backseat of my Packard for a similar reason. I expected Demeter to ball me out like I was still just a dirty kid, but she hadn't.

"'Dem, didn't you say that you had some slaughtering to do for Floyd's Anna day-of-next?" Demeter asked, pointing with her thumb and spoon in the direction of Floyd and his wife Anna.

"I suppose. She came down a while back asking on account of how I done with the last one."

"You always was a hell of a pig killer," Pa gruffed up.

"Well, maybe Trip can give you a ride tomorrow?" Demeter asked with a smile towards me.

It wasn't really a question, but I assented Demeter with a nod, poised for the jibe I knew was coming from 'Dem about whether a city car could tote a whole ham hock. But his eyes were all big and bright and his forming smile was the dead tell he was still too enraptured with Pa's offhand compliment to notice his opportunity.

"I should have been a butcher, hunh? Just drive 'round, kill what needs kill't, cut what needs cut."

Pa stayed hunched to his plate, a spoonful of butter-corn paused before his waiting mouth.

"Naw, 'Dem. You got the farm to tend, and that's got more to it than any butcher'er. You got it just like I do, and when I'm too bent with ar-riritis for any of it, I'll give it up and when you pass it on after your time you'll still be a part of it, livin' in every row you'd plowed and ditch you'd dug for your kids too."

'Dem's face looked like it might split along the wrinkles that his big dumb grin furrowed across his cheeks, and Demeter squirmed and startled, patting my arm and cooing "you got your place too, Trip."

'Dem laughed, still high on confidence. "Yeah, just not out in the country where the hicks go to dinner without our jackets and tails!" He slapped Pa's shoulder to no response.

"I've, ah …." I stood up, stuffing the hanky I'd had on my lap into the pocket of the tweed vest that matched my suit's pants, "out to school, I've got into the habit of having a smoke when I ate, and if you — Y'all excuse —" I mumbled on, fumbling with the chair and forgetting not to let the backdoor's screen slam.

The night air felt cold on my skin either from the fresh sunburn or the blushing. I rubbed pockets looking for my tobacco, knowing at once I kept in my jacket's pocket. I turned to the sound of the screen door's soft clasp to see Demeter standing cross-armed on the step staring at me.

"Quit you're poutin' and come in 'fore dinner gets cold."

"I ain't pouting."

"Like hell you ain't. Trip, I ain't never know a child who'd pout like you."

I became aware of how my lip stuck out despite myself.

"Well, I'd wouldn't a never pouted if there wasn't nothing to put about."

"What's that supposed to mean?"

She cocked her head at me, the same look a bull gives before it charges.

"You always liked 'Dem more. Ever since you came. I know neither of us is rightly yours, but you always — you held him at the tit like he was your own, and you never did for me like that."

"Oh, Trip. You was already in britches when me and your Pop came together. If I'd of held you to my tit, you'd be more right to blame me than not."

She had a womanly giggle that found a place in my throat, too, suddenly embarrassed that I'd mentioned my step-mother's breast.

"Maybe I did baby 'Dem too much. When I came out here, it was right after that no-good-sunna-bitch took my daughter and run off down south, and I was missing her something fierce, and … maybe I wanted 'Dem to be my boy some. But that's not out of spite for you."

"But the old man knows and 'Dem's getting the farm and I'm going to be just —"

"Just what? You think you got a scholarship because your Pa loved 'Dem more? You're at college and he's not because 'Dem's dumber than the dirt. Child, you going to learn things, you going to learn wonderful things, and you going to teach 'em to us dirt-dumb farmers an' folks like your Pa who grew up pushing ox and who's too scared of this new mechanical scientific farming to understand it. Why you think I said for you to take 'Dem out to Floyd's? 'Dem can butcher alright, but he can't tell why the Floyd's sow keeps losing liters."

The apology started my hung-open mouth, but first she told me to come back in because she hadn't cooked all afternoon to have the food gone cold.

***

The next morning the sun rose into a cloudless sky and cast long shadows down the rows of the field. I'd already got the top casing back on the tractor, and felt the crank start to give as I'd spread on the grease.

I wiped my hands on my jacket and rubbed the starter wheel round with my palms, one over the other, and a sputter started and then a sucking whirl. I looked to the farmhouse to see it waking as the big mechanical beast came back to life, roaring out across the fields.

Grain Mother

by Jen McConnel

Oh, great Lady,
bless us with your bounty.

Grain Mother,
we call to you
as the wheel turns.

We call to you, Mother,
seeking your smile,
with our arms open,
ready to receive.

We honor you, Demeter,
for the harvests past,
and we shall always praise
the Mother of the Grain.

The Thrice-Ploughed Field
by Suz Thackston

I move through my fields of undulating grain, fingertips trailing through the bearded grasses, hair unbound, sun warming my skin. He is there. His back is bent as he works over his plough, the oxen's shoulders moving placid and slow, the plough cutting deep into my rich, dark earth. Sweat gleams on his broad back, his hair cornsilk under the sun. I stop at the edge of the field, half-concealed amid the whispering stalks of grain, mesmerized, entranced as he urges his beasts on, working the soil, the plough turning the earth into good straight furrows, long and inviting, awaiting the seed.

My sister watched me as I left, eyeing me sidelong under her lashes, one white hand sliding along her gemmed girdle, laces loosened, proffering. I smiled at her and shook my head. No need for that, not now, not for him. We are of one mind, she and I.

He turns the oxen and they return, slow and inexorable as the seasons. The surface of the earth is dry and crumbly, but underneath it is damp and dark, fecund. Its rich scent mingles with that of the sweet grass that tickles my calves and sets me to dreaming. I see the curve of his upper arm as he manhandles the plough into the turn, the lines of his thigh muscles as he strains forward with his beasts, his teeth flashing white as he calls encouragement to them, wiping the sweat from his brow. He is golden-brown, sweet as roasted barley, and his eyes are as blue as the shallows of the Aegean.

Three times he drives his oxen the length and breadth of the field, three times the soil is raised, turned, combed, silkened, until it is soft, moist, pliable as coarse flour. He brings the team to a halt, speaks softly to them, scratches their thick necks, laughs like a boy when they rub their broad heads against him, unharnesses them, hobbles them to graze. He looks over his handiwork, stretches, sighs, smiles.

I step forth out of the tall grass.

He sees the movement, straightens, stands motionless, staring. I move toward him, my wheaten hair swirling around my hips, my green gown rippling. As I move toward him my fingers play in the ties to my golden girdle, loosen them, drawing his eyes, where they widen and fix, blue and shocked. I drift to a stop before him, my gown parting slightly, and those eyes lift to my face and meet mine, and the shock startles us both. I move swiftly forward and his warm strong arms catch me up and pull me desperately to him, his sweet sweet mouth on mine. And we fall to the receptive earth.

The ploughing is strong, the furrow deep, the seed vigorous.

As my lover nears the third sowing I see over his straining shoulders, his bright hair, the thunderheads piling up in the heavens. My heart leaps. He is coming, my brother, my lover, my lord, He who will bless this planting with fruitfulness and immortality. A few drops of rain patter down, cool drops sliding on my love's hot sweet salty skin and I taste it, exquisite. Thunder mutters softly, a gentle threat, then builds to a bellow like a great bull, even as my man rears over me and roars back at the sky, eyes closed, face contorted with divine ecstasy. And as his seed spurts forth yet again we are blinded by the God's shaft, the bolt stabbing down from the roiling chaos of clouds, impaling my love. The blue eyes fly open, stare aghast into my face, freezing my heart with the unspoken cry of terror and betrayal. I scream aloud in love and loss, and in the instant before my love is vaporized, I see those beautiful eyes light with comprehension, and his final whisper is of love and acceptance.

The thunder rolls, is muted, wanders away over the sea, lightning flashing spasmodically. I lie in the ploughed furrow, naked under the driving rain, drenched, spent, weeping, exultant.

The seed lies deep within the earth. In the turning of the seasons it sprouts, pushes forth, emerges, thrusts eagerly upward. Thousands, millions, countless polished, perfect grains, replicating themselves in the endless miracle of growth. Their mortality is essential to the immortal cycle. There are so many, so very many, mortals cannot comprehend how even a goddess can know and love them all. But each beloved seed is unique, incredible, wondrous, and is utterly known by me and held in my divine love. A love and bounty I can share with humankind because of my lost, yet eternal, immortal, infinitely precious lover, Iasion.

Harvest Prayer for Demeter

by Melia Brokaw

Hail and Praise Demeter, Mother of all that grows.
As stores are filled again with flavorful bounty,
I thank you for your generosity
which sustains both body and spirit.
The riches of vine, orchard and field
are born of your power, Harvest Mother.
Our spirits rise with your beauty,
for you are everywhere:
in meadow and mountainside,
in field and garden and all that grows.
Beloved Demeter, your mysteries of the seed
bring us the miracle of
birth, growth, death and rebirth.
As the grain was separated from the earth,
as the seed was separated from the chaff,
separate from me that which I do not need.
Help me to continue to grow
so that my full potential is reached
before I too am cut down.
Hail Lady of Mysteries.
Hail Bountiful Queen
Hail Demeter.

Hymn to Demeter II

by Rebecca Buchanan

i sing of demeter

for she is the
furrow,
rich, ripe and deep

for she is the
green shoot,
herald of spring

for she is the
poppy
amidst the grain

for she is the
barley,
life-giving wheat

for she is the
bearer
of sweet apples

for she is the
keeper
of sacred law

for she is the
veiled one,
wrathful mourning

for she is the
black mare,
implacable

for she is the
great sow,
fierce and fertile

for she is the
savior,
queen of great rites

Demeter's Kiss

by Jennifer Lawrence

We see you in the barley with which we make our daily bread;
We see you in the joy of life that keeps our spirits fed.
You come to us when Winter ends and carry in the Spring;
You lift our hearts, enchant our minds, and teach us how to sing.

Without you, we wouldn't have sweet apples, figs, or dates;
Without you, we couldn't feed our children or our mates.
Without your love, there wouldn't be a harvest or a crop,
Without your touch upon the land, the snows would never stop.

We seek your kiss in flowers and in vegetables and grain;
We know it is your magic that brings food from toil and pain.
We thank you for each blessing that you send us from above,
And honor you with laughter, and with incense, and with love.

When I kneel down to plant a seed, I feel you at my side;
I know you're watching as I tend my garden with calm pride.
I hope to please you with my labors as you guide my hand,
And spread your emerald bounty far across the fertile land.

Demeter's Daughters

by C.J. Prince

A gathering of madonnas at your breakfast table,
women in circles nurturing She Who Rests Within:
high priestess, empress, popess,
carrier of justice,
star women everywhere in circles,
dancing in moonlight,
making sand castles,
shuffling cards.

Persephone returns with the light of laughter,
her footsteps a path of daffodils sun yellow,
holy woman,
you in the mirror, in the back of the bus,
in the pulpit, on the street.
Save the world, they say —
but you cannot listen
for you are saving your world
one moment at a time.

When overwhelmed, Persephone
will help reduce the heat.
Take time in the low blue flame
to find violet, that moment
as the onions begin to simmer.
Stir with a wooden spoon before roux
blackens with neglect.

Skunk cabbage leaps
where you saunter the lake path,
green swords stretching skyward.
You hear spring call out and your holiness
expands with each heartbeat.
Does Persephone's laughter
waft on ethers
of a pollen laden breeze?

Demeter listens in as
the madonnas gather again
at your breakfast table,
glimmering like pomegranates in sunlight.
Each grain of sand that clings to bare feet,
a promise the moon will rise again
as you step along seventy-eight stairs
to archetypal wisdom.

You are the shaman growing
the world anew after a tsunami,
woman rising
with a belly full of planet earth
to birth anew Persephone's return.

My Persephone

by Jennifer Lawrence

Today my daughter came with me into the garden,
Following in the footsteps of your own child.
She knelt with me to dig holes for the peppers and the tomatoes,
Packed moist earth around the roots of the cauliflower and broccoli.
I taught her about throwing away stones that would cramp the growing potatoes,
About compost and how even things we might consider garbage
Can nourish a tender, growing thing,
And about destroying parasites before they have a chance
To hurt the vulnerable babies that we work so hard to raise.
I told her about the three things that every plant needs to thrive:
Warm sunlight on its face to urge it toward the sky,
Sweet earth cradling its core to feed it day by day,
And water poured gently all around so it might not fade and wither.
She listened soberly, face tilted toward the green shoots
That would feed us in the months to come, understanding a little
What it means to till the earth, to protect defenseless young living things

That cannot defend themselves, and so
In a way, she understands what it is to be a mother.

O Demeter, hear my prayer, as my daughter
    becomes like yours,
Sitting at my side when I kneel in supplication to
    you
Among the basil and the sage, the asparagus and the
    grapevines:
Watch over her with the same dear love you bore
    your own Persephone,
And keep her safe until it is her time
To move on and create her own garden.

Solstice Plea to Demeter

by Melia Brokaw

By the command of Zeus,
we live within the pattern of creation.
By the command of Zeus,
we are given blessings and trials.
By the command of Zeus,
a drama, a change.
All that happens, happens
because Zeus wills it to be so.
I bow to you, Father Zeus,
And praise your works.

Hestia, Lady of the Hearth, Keeper of the Flame
Wherever you are the Gods have a home
For you are the center of all
Giving warmth and comfort,
Uniting those that are estranged,
Bring peace to troubled hearts.

Demeter, tonight is the longest night of the year
A time when spring seems so very far away.
Helios has been taking his cue from you.
He has been tarrying longer and longer
In his visits with Persephone and Hades.
Tonight we ask you to bring him back to us.
Reconcile with your daughter.
Make your peace with her husband.
Remember the pomegranate,

While it is a the cause of her departure,
It also symbolizes her return.
Sooth your troubled heart.
See for yourself how she fares.
On your return, bring back Helios.
Bring back the light so that warmth can follow.
Give us a beacon of hope
as we await Kore's return.

[pause to contemplate the rising sun]

We thank you Mother,
For answering our plea yet again.
With the sun's happy return
We will gather with loved ones.
Giving and receiving hospitality
Of friend, family and stranger alike.
Sharing food, drink, laughter and gifts.
We shall celebrate your reconciliation.
We will toast Helios' return.
We look forward to the return of the light
For it heralds spring and warmth once again.

Demeter and Persephone,
Mother and Daughter,
Queen above and Queen below.
All that lives, dies.
And in turn, is born again.
All pass through their realms,
Even Helios, the sun.

For both compose the Dance of Life,
Never ending and ever changing.
Each day, each season moves the dance
Flowing seamlessly one into another.
Winter, Spring, Summer, Fall.
Life balances death.
Activity balances rest.
Growth balances fallowness.

Hestia, Lady of the Hearth, Keeper of the Flame
Wherever you are the Gods have a home
For you are the spiritual center of all.
Thank you for the warmth and comfort.
Thank you for uniting the estranged.
Thank you for giving peace to the troubled heart.
By your agency, the light will return.

Zeus, by your command
a daughter's hand was given
And a mother mourned.
By your command,
a compromise was achieved.
By your command,
Winter, spring, summer, fall.
All that happens, happens
because Zeus wills it to be so.
I bow to you, Father Zeus,
And praise your works.

<u>Semolina Quinoa</u>
<u>-- A Grain Chant in Praise of Demeter</u>

by Fern G.Z. Carr

semolina quinoa
semolina quinoa
sem sem noa noa
sem sem noa noa
flax flax flax

buckwheat emmer
buckwheat emmer
buck buck mer mer
buck buck mer mer
teff teff teff

amaranth bulgur
amaranth bulgur
ama ran bul bul
ama ran bul bul
spelt spelt spelt

wild rice triticale
wild rice triticale
wild wild trit trit
wild wild trit trit
bran bran bran

sorghum millet
sorghum millet

ghum ghum mill mill
ghum ghum mill mill
oats oats oats

barley canola
barley canola
bar bar ola ola
bar bar ola ola
rye rye rye

*Quinoa is pronounced keen - wah.

Seeds

by Rebecca Buchanan

"Welcome to the People's Republic of Alaska, Ms. Bud .... Budz .... Bud ...." The clerk scowled down at the ipass laid flat on the desk.

"Budziszewski," Melania supplied helpfully. She pulled up the corners of her mouth in a vague smile and widened her eyes, hoping for innocent and guileless.

"Hhmm." The clerk turned his scowl on her, finger tapping the page icon in the corner of the ipass. He glanced back down as the screen flipped from one port of entry stamp to another. "Republic of Ukraine, the Baltic Commonwealth, Armenia, Moldova, and hunh — " one eyebrow shot up " — the Restored Christian Kingdom of Finland. You have visited some very ... interesting places since departing from Poland, Ms. Bud ... Budzi ... ma'am."

"Yes, my work does require quite a bit of travel." She tilted her head, eyes still wide. "Honestly, though, I am sure none of those places are nearly as interesting or beautiful as your Republic. I was hoping to see the ruins of Juneau once I concluded my business. Are tours still being offered?"

Melania felt the man behind her shift restlessly. The line of tourists, immigrants, and refugees continued to grow. Luggage rattled. Sighing and grumbling and shushing of children. Overhead, voices in a dozen different languages called out flight information and repeatedly reminded travelers of food restrictions, inoculation requirements, curfews, and quarantines.

The clerk pursed his lips. "That's south — "

"I was afraid it might be too late in the season, that the city might be totally underwater," she prattled on. "If not Juneau, perhaps an indigenous experience. A bear hunt or elk — "

The clerk's eyes bounced back and forth between Melania and the shifting, restless line. "Um, yes."

"How messy do those get, though?" Melania knit her eyebrows together, going for a perplexed look. "I mean, yucky? I don't — "

"Yes, thank you." The clerk pressed his thumb to the screen and there was a soft bleep. Then he pressed down the digistamp; for a moment, the symbol of the People's Republic of Alaska glowed on the screen. The clerk flipped the cover closed and the ipass went into sleep mode with a pook-pook. He held out the small tablet. "Enjoy your stay, and please come again. Next!"

The man behind Melania impatiently shoved around her, pushing her to the side. She kept the vague smile on her face, murmuring a "thank you" of her own. Ipass clutched tightly in one hand, rolling suitcase in the other, she headed for the next gauntlet.

One more security gate, she reminded herself. Just one more.

Her luggage bumped over a crack in the tile. She tightened her grip on the handle and pulled into line behind a pale, thin woman with four thin, unruly children. The woman's shoulders drooped with exhaustion. Head bound in a white turban, floor-length white dress, no jewelry, no make-up. Neo-Islamist. Likely a refugee from the Pure Land of the Faithful. No husband, either. Dead, or perhaps she had managed to flee without him. Or from him.

Inch by inch, she drew closer to the gate. Guards in black and yellow swarmed, and bright red warning signs covered every flat surface and hung from the ceiling. No undocumented fauna beyond this point. No unlicensed agricultural products beyond this point. No print information beyond this point. Illegal electronics will be confiscated and destroyed.

She tried not to stare at the exit. Through the plexiglass, the day glowed a hard, cold white.

One of the children twisted his head around and glanced at her, eyes dull. Her lips tilted up in a sincere smile. He blinked at her. Digging into her coat pocket, Melania pulled out a protein bar. It was still sealed; her stomach had been too knotted with tension for her to eat. She held out the bar. The boy's eyes widened for a moment before narrowing in suspicion. She opened her hand, palm flat. Small fingers darted out, snatching the bar away. The boy twisted around, and she heard the wrapper being torn open. The other children huddled close, munching and mmming. Her eyes stung as she realized that he was sharing the protein bar with his brother and sisters.

Steps sluggish, the children's mother took no notice.

Another inch. Another inch. Another. Melania waved her ipass, fanning her face as sweat beaded along the top of her forehead.

The exhausted mother and her brood reached the gate. Melania waited at the bright white line while the security guards patted the woman, hands rough and thorough. The children cringed and twisted at the strangers touching them; the youngest whined. Their few pieces of luggage were opened, the contents spread out on tables and examined. Handheld x-ray scanners were brought over, and thermal scanners, and a pair of toothy, hulking german shepherds.

Throat tight, face aching from holding her vague smile in place, Melania exhaled slowly as the family was finally waved through the gate. One of the security guards — tall, blonde, face etched with deep lines — lifted a hand. Melania surrendered her ipass, tamping down the urge to start babbling.

"Name?" The blonde's voice was toneless, distant.

"Melania Katzienska Budziszewski."

A female guard, dark hair pulled back into a tight bun, pistols strapped to either hip, stepped over. She started at Melania's head and worked her way down, pinching, patting, squeezing, poking. Melania forced herself not to flinch, not to twist away.

"Business?"

"Jewelry. Design and distribution for Saada-Favret International."

Pistols wrinkled her nose, leaning in close. She lifted the chain around Melania's neck, pulling the pendant free from where she had tucked it beneath her blouse. The guard flipped it over in her hand, front, back, front, back, front, back, and Melania lost control of her tongue.

"An old coin I picked up in a bazaar in Macedonia. That's Demeter holding a sheaf of wheat — " she pointed " — and Victory on the other side. The vendor said it was a good luck piece, and it certainly has brought me luck. See how the green frame complements the gold of the coin, and the variegated shading of the green beads woven into the chain — "

"Yeah, yeah, nice." Pistols dropped the pendant.

"Allotted duration of stay?" Blonde continued.

"Six days."

He flipped the ipass shut. "Be aware that residency beyond the legally allowed six days is a felony and that conviction will result in a mandatory five year sentence, to be served on the Kodiak Penal Colony. You must keep your ipass on your person at all times, and be prepared to present it to any law enforcement officer upon request. Failure to do so ...."

Melania's attention drifted, her eyes sliding over to the examination tables. Blue-gloved guards dug through her single suitcase, poking and prodding. Fabric ripped. Dogs sniffed.

A tablet appeared in front of her.

"Sign here that you have been advised of and understand your alien visitant rights." Blonde's voice was still flat and disinterested.

Melania ran her finger across the screen, her signature a series of a barely-legible loops and arcs.

"Thank you and enjoy your stay."

Her suitcase was dumped back at her feet; one red blouse, caught and mangled by the zipper, poked out of a corner. The left front wheel wobbled.

Blonde pointed at the exit.

Lips in a tight smile, eyes wide, Melania walked slowly towards the door.

***

Melania pressed her nose to the cab's window, squinting against the bright light. Slush sprayed the side of the car. Pedestrians scurried, heads down.

Armed police stood on corners and zipped around in striped black and yellow cruisers.

At least there were fewer police here than there had been in Finland ....

Melania shivered, pulling the collar of her coat up higher around her neck. She leaned back a bit, studying the city, comparing what she saw to what she had been told in encrypted emails. As the oceans rose, Juneau and other coastal cities were largely abandoned, and the capital was relocated to Fairbanks. The city's population swelled as native Alaskans, and refugees from the former Lower Forty-Eight and farther afield sought relief from storms, rising temperatures, rising waters, and erratic food supplies. Permanent, semi-permanent, and temporary shelters spread across the Tanana Valley, right up to the very fence of the airport and all the way around. The Tanana River was a sluggish dark blue, just beginning to ice over; anyone who did not escape the temporary shelters within the next month would freeze to death. Shallow hills and valleys rolled off to the east and west, while treacherous marsh and bog spread almost two hundred kilometers to the south, right into the foothills of the Alaska Range.

The cab slowed and pulled beneath the archway of the Midnight Sun Hotel and 24-Hour Eatery. The doors swooshed open and shut as guests came and went, hefting backpacks and babies and bags of leftovers. Melania caught a whiff of soy burgers and stale bread.

Swiping her credit card through the taxi's built-in reader, she thanked the driver and headed inside. The lobby was small, a neat-looking clerk behind the counter along the left wall. The restaurant lay straight ahead through a pair of french doors, while stuffed chairs and a coffee stand were to the right. Melania slowed, pretending to dig through her pockets, and allowed her gaze to drift over the seating area. Three people: a Caucasian man in a battered red baseball cap, sound asleep; a middle-aged Hispanic woman with her face pressed too close to a tablet; and a white-haired, heavily bearded dark-skinned man yammering into his cell phone in ... Yoruba? Igbo? Something from north-central Africa.

The sleeping man peeked at her through slitted eyes.

Melania pulled off her coat and slung it over her left arm.

The sleeping man shifted, crossing his left leg over his right.

Contact.

***

Her belly still in knots, she spent the night half-watching bad Alaskan state television: sanitized news, nature documentary, sanitized news, oil drilling reality show, sanitized news, sanitized comedy, sanitized news. Not one word about the famines in Asia, the locusts swarming through the Middle East, or the fields of hyper-aggressive wheat consuming the rain forests of Brazil. Sometime around three in the morning, she finally fell asleep, arm bent awkwardly beneath her head, television flickering.

The phone squealed at seven in the am, the clerk informing her — in clipped, efficient tones — that curfew had been lifted and that she was free to enjoy Fairbanks' many delights. Followed by a reminder that failure to return before curfew was reinstated at five in the evening would result in mandatory incarceration and confiscation of her ipass.

Melania slammed down the receiver, pulled the pillow over her head, and went back to sleep.

Anxiety and hunger soon drove her into the bathroom. She stood in the freezing shower, teeth chattering, stomach cramping. A screen built into the wall flashed ads for local museums, massage parlors, historical tours, and hunting expeditions; reminded her that possession of illegal pharmaceuticals, foodstuffs, electronic devices, and books was a felony; and promised a hot shower in exchange for a (not insignificant) surcharge. As soon as her hair was clean and her body scrubbed, Melania hopped out, dried off, wrapped herself in her robe, and crawled back under the covers to warm up.

Purse banging against her hip, ipass tucked carefully inside her jacket, she made it downstairs just as the free continental breakfast was closing. She snatched away the remaining three soy sausages, two reconstituted powdered eggs, and a carton of hazelnut milk before the kitchen staff could dump them in tubs for recycling; her scarf dragged through the margarine. Mouth full of sausage, she balanced the remaining food on a napkin and headed out the door. She ignored the desk clerk, who peered over her glasses at Melania, lips pulled into a moue of disapproval.

The encrypted emails had been brief. *Sleep beneath the midnight sun. Watch for the left-legged man. Treasures in the ice. Uncle William is a dirty man.* Tucking her scarf inside her jacket, she pulled up her hood and ducked into one of the waiting cabs. She reminded herself to smile at the driver. "Museum of the North, U of A campus, please."

***

First established in 1911, the museum had outgrown two buildings over the decades, before a recent purge reduced it to a fraction of its former glory. Students huddled on benches here and there, some with books open, some sleeping. Police patrolled the corridors, narrow-eyed. A docent, voice filled with forced cheerfulness, led a gaggle of tourists from one room to the next, describing the wonders of the People's oil-fueled Republic.

Melania attached herself to the back of one such group, a mixture of Russians, Canadians and Brits to judge by their accents and clothing. A bored teenage boy stepped on her foot; he mumbled an apology. She ignored him, pretending to listen to the docent while her eyes darted back and forth, around, around, searching each room as they entered it.

Then, finally, finally, in the totem room — there. The African man from the Midnight Sun. He stood near one wall, scowling at a totem. He turned as the tour group entered, dark eyes briefly brushing across her own. He grimaced and scratched his left thigh.

Melania moved her purse onto her left shoulder.

Steps casual, he walked towards the front doors, pausing occasionally to flip through his brochure and study an exhibit. Melania followed, dawdling when necessary to keep some distance between them. The doors whooshed behind him and, by the time she stepped out onto the sidewalk, he was most of the way across the quad.

The wind kicked up. She tightened her scarf, shoved her hands in her pockets, and tried not to run.

***

They walked for nearly an hour. He led her in a roundabout circuit, up one block and back down the next. When a police cruiser wailed and pulled up beside her, she tightened her stomach, smiled, flirted and handed over her ipass for inspection. Out of the corner of her eye, she saw the African man pause in front of a restaurant to study the menu posted in the window. The police wished her well, waved her on her way, and drove off.

Teeth chattering, she shoved her hands back in her pockets. He let her get within half a block before he started walking again. A hard right, two more blocks, then a left into a mixed residential/commercial district. A few buildings down, he stepped beneath an awning and through a plexiglass door. She slowed her steps, casting quick glances up and down the street. Only a couple of pedestrians. She tilted her head back, studying the building as she passed in front of it. Florescent green letters in the front windows identified it as Bill's Recycling Services (We Take The Trash Other Guys Won't!).

She stepped beneath the awning. One more quick look around and she shoved through the door.

The smell hit her and she almost backpedaled right out again. Eyes watering, nose twitching, she headed across the grimy floor, around piles of rubber and scrap steel and copper wires, towards the counter. It was cracked and yellowed. A short, thin brown-skinned man — indigenous Alaskan to judge by his features — sat hunched over the counter, sorting through piles of aluminum cans and lids. A barely-legible name tag sewn on the front of his shirt read "Bill."

Melania pulled a shallow breath in through her mouth, tasting oil and metal and rotten food. "Morning. Quite a coincidence. My uncle is named Bill, too ... except we usually call him William."

Bill stopped sorting. He tossed one last lid onto the pile on his right and looked up at her. He studied her for a long moment, before a slow smile spread across his face, warming his skin and eyes. Melania found herself smiling back. He thrust out a dirty hand and she found his grip firm and dry. "Welcome to Fairbanks. Have any trouble?"

"No more than usual. Would the People's Republic of Alaska be offended if I said your security was less intimidating than Finland's?"

Bill snorted a laugh. "Probably." He stood, walking around the counter towards a curtained doorway. "Come on back." He pushed aside the curtain, revealing a solid metal door and keypad. Melania kept her eyes carefully averted as he entered the code. "You done this often enough to know the rules?" The lock pinged and metal scrapped as the heavy bolts released.

Melania nodded. "Given names only. No locations. No names of secondary contacts. Absolutely no discussion of the vaults. But, good tricks for getting passed security are always appreciated."

Bill threw a grin at her over his shoulder as he shoved the door open. He waved her in and she found herself face to face with the white-bearded African man. He dipped his head in greeting as Bill introduced them. "Achebe, Melania. Melania, Achebe."

Melania bowed her head in turn. "Nice to meet you."

"Come," Achebe intoned. "The others are waiting."

***

The Fairbanks cell was careful. Achebe led her down a short corridor to another locked metal door, through an empty storage room, through a half-rotten wooden door and up a steep set of stairs, down another corridor lined with numbered doors and back down a flight of carpeted steps. They were in a completely different building, she realized, but which one she wasn't sure. Around a couple of corners to another wooden door. Achebe knocked twice, then again.

The door opened. The man from the Midnight Sun, red cap stuffed into his jacket pocket, waved them inside. He stuck his head out into the corridor, looked around quickly, then closed the door, sliding two chains and three bolts into place. "Folks, say hello to Melania."

She loosened her scarf, smiling and nodding at the chorus of greetings. The apartment was small, just a living area with a stone fireplace, kitchen along one wall, bedroom through one door, bathroom through another. Cast-off, mismatched chairs and a love seat and a low table filled the space, but there were fuzzy blankets and area rugs and overstuffed pillows in a dozen different colors and the fireplace was warm and the faint scent of strawberries and rhubarb hung in the air.

Baseball Cap waved his hand at the half dozen people perched and sprawled across that mismatched furniture. "Melania, please meet Marguerite, Keshi, Flor, Alexander, and Aabheer. You know Achebe, and I'm Thom."

Melania unzipped her jacket and flexed her cold fingers. "Hello." Middle-aged white woman of unknown nationality; a very young woman of Japanese origin; a thin Hispanic woman with a decorative comb in her white hair and bruised, spotted skin; a mustachioed man, possibly Greek; and a Hindi man with golden-brown skin and liquid brown eyes. Melania tried not to sniffle as her nose and face warmed.

"We should get started," Achebe suggested, gingerly lowering himself beside Alexander. "We need to get back before curfew."

"Right." Thom grabbed a handful of small metal trays and a green candle. After setting a tray down in front of each of them, he placed the candle in the middle of the low table, lit it, then plopped down onto the floor near Marguerite. "Flor, as the eldest, you have the place of honor."

Flor nodded, holding out her hands to Keshi and Alexander on either side. Melania took the chair (wood badly scratched, seat soft blue cotton) beside Achebe. His hand was dry and calloused and much larger than her own; she felt a scar running across the bottom of his palm.

"Pachamama," Flor intoned, voice soft, "who gifted us with seeds and taught us to plant and to harvest and to keep the earth, in your name I share your gifts."

"For the Savior born in poverty," whispered Alexander, "who walked the world, breathing the air that I breathe, drinking the water that I drink. In your name, I hold these secret things safe."

"For Okko," Achebe began, "orisha of all good growing things, and Ozain, keeper of the herbs which sweeten life. In your name, I keep your gifts safe, and share them with those who understand."

"Demeter, mother of all good grains and the poppy." Melania felt her throat catch. Her nose was starting to run. "In your name, I protect these precious gifts, sharing them only with a trusted few, until the time is right."

She squeezed Aabheer's hand and he smiled at her. "For Bhūmi, aspect of Lakshmi, who holds in her hands the pomegranate and the lotus. In your name, I share these precious gifts, trusting your chosen to keep them safe."

Thom wrinkled his nose, apparently trying to hold in a sneeze. They all giggled. Flushing slightly, Thom continued the invocation. "For the mighty spirits of frost and earth and air: Akna the mother, Pinga the huntress and healer, Qailertetang of the dancing skies, Sedna of the deep seas. In honor and fear of you, I hold these secrets close."

Marguerite sighed, eyes closed. "Abellio, who gifted us with the apple tree so that we might make wonderful pies — " chuckling and giggling from the group " — and Erecura who bears the cornucopia, and sun-warmed Nantosuelta: in honor of you, I share your gifts."

Finally, Keshi spoke, eyes downcast. "For Inari Okami and Uke Mochi, whose gifts must be hidden from those who do not understand."

Silence, for a long moment.

Thom released Aabheer and Marguerite's hands, inviting Flor to lead them again. "What did you bring?"

Flor pulled the comb loose and her long white hair tumbled across her shoulders and down her back. Leaning forward over the table, she unscrewed one tooth of the comb, and tipped it over the tray. Brilliant pink seeds rained onto the metal. "Huautli, from high in the Andes."

Achebe, then, who ripped open the sole of his left shoe. Grinning widely, he set three small plastic sleeves on the tray in front of him. "I made a few stops on my way here. Ebony acorn squash and pink banana jumbo squash and painted serpent cucumber." Marguerite applauded, practically bouncing in her seat, and Thom was nodding.

Melania swallowed, sliding her ipass from her pocket. "Does anyone have a knife I can borrow?"

"Oh, yeah, sure." Thom clambered to his feet, dug around in a kitchen drawer for a moment, then handed her a jackknife. "Need a permit to own that. Otherwise, three years on Kodiak."

Alexander snorted.

Flicking open the knife, Melania held the ipass close to her chest. Carefully powering it down, she pulled the cover off, the magnetic clasps releasing with a shnikt. Tucking the ipass back inside her jacket, she set the cover on the table and carefully slipped the tip of the blade into the seam. Running it around the edge, slowly, she peeled back the top of the cover. Inside lay four nearly-flat plastic bags with tiny seeds. She named the seeds as she picked up each bag and set it in the tray. "White albino beet. Giant nobel spinach. Velvet queen sunflower. Roman chamomile."

And around they went, until the trays were filled with precious treasures. Cinnamon basil. Danish ballhead cabbage. Hearts of gold melon. Tiger tomato. Cherry vanilla quinoa. Painted daisy. California bluebell. Crimson clover. Red clover. Early purple sprouting broccoli.

Eyes wide, Marguerite stared at the table. "I don't think I've ever — I mean, there's just so much. So much variety. I don't think I've seen this much outside a seed vault. Oops!" She slapped a hand over her mouth as Keshi shot her a glare. "I shouldn't have said that."

"It's all right," Melania assured her, studying the table. The seeds were deep red and pale white and yellow and deep black, round and oblong and tear-shaped. Some were so tiny that dozens fit into a single plastic sleeve, while others were only two or three to a bag. "It's beautiful. It's wonderful."

"Makes me angry, to think what we have lost," Keshi scowled.

"Yes," Flor nodded. "Which is why we are here. To save what we can, because we are angry, and because we have hope. Ancient treasures, saved for the future."

Another long silence. The fire snapped.

Finally, Melania sighed. "Very well, then. I can take some of the cherry vanilla quinoa and huautli, the bluebell and daisy, too." She looked around the circle, at these, her comrades in conscience and faith. "What can everyone else take?"

***

" ... And, oh my gosh, the museums are amazing! Have you been? Simply amazing! You totally need to go — "

"Yes, ma'am." The clerk sighed, hair pulled back so tightly into a bun that her face stretched. Overhead, the speakers blared, calling out flight information, and quarantine and embargo reminders.

" — so much amazing history. I really wish I could have gone on a tour of Juneau, but — "

"Yes, ma'am. Thank you, ma'am." The clerk shoved the ipass at Melania. "All stamped, hope you enjoyed your stay in the People's Republic of Alaska, please come again, next!"

"Oh, thank you." Melania smiled, slipping the ipass carefully into her inside jacket pocket. Her fingers brushed across the pendant, carefully tucked beneath her blouse. "Perhaps I will, some day."

Thalusia Hymn

by Sannion

Welcome to our plentiful feast O august Deo,

grandmother of the vine and wet-nurse of mountain-fostered Bakcheios,

you who love the season of autumn when the golden wheat is threshed

and the leaves on the fair trees burn brightest before they fall

and the last of the produce is brought to market by the industrious farmers,

those holy toilers in the fields who keep your traditions alive with their tireless labor

feeding the city of the well-born ones in this fertile valley

nourished by the pure waters of the Willamette and McKenzie rivers.

O frenzied Chloê, accept this offering we gathered for you

and carried home in the liknon-basket, all the best fruits, grains and vegetables we could find.

May the fragrance of fresh-baked bread be pleasing to you O mistress Demeter,

you who first taught man to cultivate the earth and make food from plants

instead of the flesh of beasts; you who caused us to put aside our savage ways

and embrace just laws and the harmonious existence of civilized city-life.

You with eyes like blue camas flowers and hair green as hops, crowned with poppies,

you who hold barley in your hands to remind us of that wonderful beverage, dear to your heart,

that you first quenched your thirst with when you searched for your beautiful daughter over the whole earth.

Rejoice O bountiful Ceres in our celebration,

as we rejoice in all that you have graciously bestowed upon us

and we will remember you again next year!

First Fruits Festival Prayer

by Melia Brokaw

Hail Demeter and Kore
The seeds have ripened,
Your promise has come to fruition,
Heralding the change of seasons.
Soon greenery in field, mountain and meadow
Shall perish in winter's cold
Foretelling Kore's return to her beloved.
The cycle of life continues.
I rejoice at my good fortune,
Blessed by your bounty.
May I find joy in the simple pleasures of life:
    A child's laugh
    A kiss truly given
    A job well done
    A pantry of surety.
For these and all your gifts
I give you, Mother and Daughter, my thanks.
I also praise Zeus and all others
Whose gifts and blessings
Aided Demeter's fertile power,
For she does not work alone.
I ask for blessings on those
That work the land
And the couriers too
As they provide the food for my table.
Hail Demeter and Kore!

Song to My Mother
by Janine Canan

The Earth is my Mother.
The wind is my Mother's breath.
Trees, flowers, birds and animals —
All are my beloved Mother.

The waves are my Mother's cheeks.
The stones are my Mother's feet.
Trees, flowers, birds and animals —
All are my beloved Mother.

The stars are my Mother's crown.
The sun and moon are her eyes.
Trees, flowers, birds and animals —
All are my beloved Mother.

Demeter's Lament for Demophoön

by P. Sufenas Virius Lupus

I wail and mourn for infant in the fire —
his kinsmen's hope, Demophoön was styled —
he can no more to deathlessness aspire.

His godly altar, now funeral pyre:
immortal silence his mother defiled ...
I wail and mourn for infant in the fire.

His blood from heroes now cannot go high'r
as when the Giants' mountain stairs were piled —
he can no more to deathlessness aspire.

With naught but flame and ambrosial attire
he would become more excellent a child ...
I wail and mourn for infant in the fire.

"Burn hot to cause Hephaistos to perspire!"
the flames of godliness I sang and riled ...
he can no more to deathlessness aspire.

I his nursemaid, good Keleos his sire,
in my disguise his family beguiled ...
I wail and mourn for infant in the fire.

Not like the mortals whose lifespans expire
was he to be, my foster-son so mild —
he can no more to deathlessness aspire.

Upon the ranks of gods he'll not run wild;
I thought from Zeus' presence to retire
and on this mortal family's fate I smiled,
all honors humankind might then acquire,
but her son's transformation was reviled ...

My turn, grandchild of Gaia, came in gyre ...

Now many death in darkness soon shall mire --
yet, perhaps to heights greater I'll inspire
when mystery rites right here are compiled ...
I wail and mourn for infant in the fire —
he can no more to deathlessness aspire.

Demeter's Other Children: Demophoön and the Eleusinian Mysteries

by P. Sufenas Virius Lupus

Though Demeter is most often credited with being the mother of the goddess Persephone, Greek tradition is rarely univocal on such genealogical matters, and thus a variety of other children are suggested for her in a variety of sources.[1] The Orphic Hymn to Eleusinian Demeter goes as far as to say "You are an only daughter, but you have many children."[2] But parental roles are not limited to one's own offspring; fosterage and being a wet-nurse are likewise regarded as intimate and parental relationships for those who undergo them. Earlier in the same Orphic Hymn, Demeter is also called "O holy and youth-nurturing lover / of children and of fair offspring,"[3] which indicates that Demeter could be regarded as many other goddesses as a kourotrophos, a "nurturer of children" for humans, both heroic and more pedestrian. It is the very particular relationship of fosterage which Demeter shares with her adopted mortal child Demophoön during her divine exile at Eleusis with which the present study is concerned, and what this may indicate not only about the Eleusinian Mysteries, but what it further highlights as a point often taken for granted when looking at the story of Demeter and Persephone. This latter point is drawn out by an examination of its oldest known narrative form of

Demeter and Persephone's story, from the *Homeric Hymn to Demeter*.

In order to understand the fullest implications of the present course of inquiry, we need to first examine the *Homeric Hymn to Demeter* itself,[4] and the important sequence of events which arises from it and lends the greater import of those events their particular gravity. In the *Homeric Hymn to Demeter*, the goddess has come to earth in her self-imposed exile from the gods, and in her fruitless search for her daughter, she has paused and taken up residence at Eleusis with the court of the king Keleos and his family, as a nurse for his infant son Demophoön. She begins the process of immortalizing the child by anointing him with ambrosia and placing him in the fire at night, magically preserving his life and preparing him for a future divine existence. This plan is thwarted when Metaneira, the wife of Keleos and the mother of Demophoön, enters the chamber where Demeter is carrying out her ritual of immortalization one night, and disrupts it, causing a sharp reproach from Demeter herself. Demophoön is turned over to lesser nurses, and king Keleos orders a temple to be built in honor of the goddess Demeter. After this, the following occurs:

> ... Then golden-haired Demeter
> remained sitting apart from all the immortals,

>   wasting with desire for her deep-girt daughter.
>   For mortals she ordained a terrible and brutal year
>   on the deeply fertile earth. The ground released
>   no seed, for bright-crowned Demeter kept it buried.
>   In vain the oxen dragged many curved plows down
>   the furrows. In vain much white barley fell on the earth.
>   She would have destroyed the whole mortal race
>   by cruel famine and stolen the glorious honor of gifts
>   and sacrifices from those having homes on Olympus,
>   if Zeus had not seen and pondered their plight in his heart.[5]

In most of the modern brief retellings and understandings of the story of Demeter and Persephone, the incident of Demophoön and the people of Eleusis is generally elided over, downplayed, or forgotten, and instead it is inferred that when Persephone was raped by Hades, Demeter's sorrow caused an immediate famine and cessation of vegetative processes on the earth. This is not the case at all: the loss of Persephone has no direct impact on these processes, and thus her actual initial rape and loss to Demeter has no role to play in the etiology of the seasons.[6] The actuality is that the famine brought on the human inhabitants of the earth is a result of Demeter's upset at having her plans to immortalize Demophoön disrupted.[7] Thus, the profound sadness she had at her own divine daughter's disappearance was heightened by this failure to secure a divine foster-child from her situation at Eleusis. It only became a concern of the gods when the famine amongst mortals endangered the offerings and sacrifices that the gods enjoyed that Zeus took action, and eventually restored Persephone to her mother.

This understanding of the actual chronology of events, and thus the importance of Demophoön to Demeter, is overlooked and underplayed far more often than it ought to be. But, we might ask why it is that Demeter mourned and was in greater anger over the loss of a mortal foster-son. In addition to pointing out the importance of this general situation and the significance of Demophoön, Sarah Iles Johnston suggested a potential answer in a presentation at PantheaCon in San Jose, California on Saturday morning, Feburary 18th of 2012.[8] Her suggestion was that perhaps Demeter's intent with Demophoön was not merely a surrogate or transitional child to temporarily fulfill the role that her lost daughter did for her in terms of nurturance and protection, but instead that she may have intended to immortalize Demophoön in order to pose a challenge to the divine sovereignty of Zeus. This notion is echoed by Helene P. Foley,[9] and by Jenny Strauss Clay.[10] Demophoön can serve both as a model for the future initiates of the Eleusinian Mysteries in honor of Demeter, but likewise, the failure of the goddess to immortalize him and bring about his apotheosis creates the necessity for the Mysteries as a kind of second-class replacement of sorts.[11]

Indeed, it might be appropriate for an earth goddess like Demeter, in her generation of divine descent, to be the impetus behind a potential divine coup to oust Zeus from the kingship. It was Gaia who incited her Titan children to overthrow Ouranos,[12] and it was the machinations of Rhea (with help from her mother Gaia) which allowed for Zeus not to be swallowed by his father Kronos, and to eventually overthrow him.[13] The use of a sickle as an instrument of sacrifice in the ritual known as the Chthonia for Demeter in Hermione, according to Johnston, is suggestive of the role the sickle played in the overthrow of Ouranos.[14] The importance of the sickle in agricultural activity as well as in certain rituals in Demeter's honor, and the coincidence of agriculture's teaching to humanity and Demeter's temple, Mysteries, and honoring in Eleusis, further suggests that perhaps at some point, had Demophoön lived, he may have been "given the sickle" by Demeter to do his work on her behalf against the elder generation of gods.

As it happens, though, Demophoön's full divinization did not take place. Instead, he ended up becoming a minor hero at Eleusis,[15] despite the general lack of iconography and apparent direct connection to him that is known in terms of the rituals at Eleusis. And yet, the ritual of the yearly young male "hearth initiate" which was enacted as a part of the Mysteries may indeed be the element that was carried through in honor of Demophoön.

If deification was not possible for humans at Demeter's hands at Eleusis, perhaps the better lot in the afterlife that the Eleusinian initiates attained was not a second-best option. Instead, it may have been a preparation for a longer-term plot on the part of Demeter to have her own retinue of mortals on her side. Such initiates, her further foster-children like Demophoön, who would be saved from the tyranny of death and habitation in her brother and son-in-law Hades' realm, would indeed be grateful to her for their better and more favored fate, and a potentially powerful "army" of sorts that might be drawn upon in some future situation.[16] We cannot be certain, in any case, but the possibility that such teachings might have been a part of the Eleusinian Mysteries remains intriguing.

Notes
1. For a summary of these, see http://www.theoi.com/Olympios/DemeterFamily.html#Divine , and also Apostolos N. Athanassakis and Benjamin M. Wolkow (ed./trans.), *The Orphic Hymns* (Baltimore: The Johns Hopkins University Press, 2013), pp. 143-148.
2. Athanassakis and Wolkow, p. 36, line 17.
3. Athanassakis and Wolkow, p. 36, lines 14-15.
4. I am using the text and translation of this Hymn from Helene P. Foley (ed./trans.), *The Homeric Hymn to Demeter: Translation, Commentary, and Interpretive Essays* (Princeton: Princeton University Press, 1994).
5. Foley, pp. 16-19, lines 302-313.
6. Foley, pp. 98-100; Jean Rudhardt, "Concerning the Homeric Hymn to Demeter," trans. Lavinia Lorch and Helene P. Foley, in Helene P. Foley (ed./trans.), *The Homeric Hymn to Demeter: Translation, Commentary, and Interpretive Essays* (Princeton: Princeton University Press, 1994), pp. 198-211 at 207.
7. Foley, p. 92.
8. Sarah Iles Johnston, "Dark Demeter, Women and Harvest," PantheaCon (San Jose, CA), 9:00 AM Saturday, February 18, 2012. Two articles upon which this presentation was based were subsequently published: "Demeter in Hermione: Sacrifice and Ritual Polyvalence," *Arethusa* 45.2 (Spring 2012), pp. 211-241; and "Demeter, Myths, and the Polyva-

lence of Festivals," *History of Religions* 52.4 (May 2013), pp. 370-401. However, none of these followed up on her suggestion, to be discussed subsequently.

9. Foley, p. 113 and n104.

10. Jenny Strauss Clay, *The Politics of Olympus: Form and Meaning in the Major Homeric Hymns* (London: Bristol Classical Press/Gerald Duckworth & Co., Ltd., 2006), pp. 202-266.

11. Ibid; Foley, pp. 48-50, 83, 101, 114, 138, 173; Nancy Felson-Rubin and Harriet M. Deal, "Some Functions of the Demophoön Episode in the Homeric Hymn to Demeter," in Helene P. Foley (ed./trans.), *The Homeric Hymn to Demeter: Translation, Commentary, and Interpretive Essays* (Princeton: Princeton University Press, 1994), pp. 190-197 at 195.

12. Apostolos N. Athanassakis (ed./trans.), Hesiod, *Theogony, Works and Days, Shield* (Baltimore: The Johns Hopkins University Press, 1983), p. 17.

13. Athanassakis, Hesiod, pp. 24-25.

14. Johnston, "Demeter, Myths"; "Demeter at Hermione." Sickles were also used, amongst other occasions, for Perseus to behead Medusa, for Herakles to behead the Lernean Hydra, and for Zeus to defeat Typhon.

15. Corinne Ondine Pache, *Baby and Child Heroes in Ancient Greece* (Urbana and Chicago: University of Illinois Press, 2004), pp. 66-83.

16. Such a potentially eschatological situation echoes the Norse myth of Ragnarok, and the army of worthy human warriors amassed by Odin in preparation for that battle.

Potnia-Ge (Our Lady of the Earth)

by Katie Anderson

Rhea-Demeter-Ge,
we move in circles,
our feet upon the earth
and our eyes fixed on the stars.
Looking back into our ancient past
before we danced your serpentine paths,
before our mothers carried your axes to war,
before you came of age,
Our great matron Demeter,
Lady of the Earth,
you joined your mothers there,
at the crossroads where earth, sea and sky once met.

Your mysteries show us the path,
that only we may walk,
as we wind around the labyrinths of our lives,
in earthly succession.
The death we shed,
and the life reborn.
The stages of our lives ever in motion,
in a state of creative urge,
Self-fulfilled,
and self-sustained,
we are as earth, sea and sky,
and where we meet
are the sacred works that none may tear asunder.

Mysteries of life and death,
as we guard the gates,
we are as guardian spirits,
charged with a forgotten inheritance,
as old and integral as the blood we shed.
These things we have taught our daughters,
the gifts given by our mothers,
without ever uttering one word,
Genetic secrets spell the epic tales
of our engendered bloodlines.

We are the mysteries of the Earth,
our hands open the gates
and our voices call you to witness
the journey taken
by all who pass through
our hearts and minds,
our bodies and souls,
in whom we have birthed
your beauty, grace, and valor.

Rhea-Demeter-Ge,
you remind us
that every generation demands
the strength of the earth,
the courage of a goddess
to face the work,
you have called us to perform.
May all that walk in your light,
ever seek to know you.

Hymn to Demeter Europa

by Lykeia

Hail Demeter, Divine Europa, O bull-mounted
>Queen
You who bear the blessed riches upon your saffron
>knee,
As plentiful grains fall endlessly from your blessed
>lap
That all mankind raises up supplicant hands to grasp
To bring his soul the bliss of divine peace and
>happiness
The holy bride, which every soul so longs to
>possess.
O venerable mother that you are, in truth, a kindly
>nurse
Let all nations laud you with loud song, O blessed
>cow of Zeus
For you succor all the tribes that range the broad
>earth
And alike you bless both noble and humble, house
>and hearth;
Just as you nursed in your fire the noble child of
>Eleusis
And in Phocis reared the son of Apollon, fair
>Delphus,
For you disparage not against any goodly house
>Through which you pass with golden feet
But with wheat and honey you relieve sorrows ….
>By your bounty of the blessed and the sweet,

And bear forth, in dark winter, Iakkhos, your son,
    from the earth
The ivied calf, just as the Thessalian maid bore the
    bull of worth.
To him your shining twins, obscurely born, in
    gleaming arraignments
Crowned in myrtle and laurel, by torches lead a
    chorus of initiates.
O Euboleus, O Misa, O Apollon, O Artemis, for you
    they sing
That every soul speeds like an arrow born on
    immortal wings;
As from your lips fall golden utterances to grace the
    race of man
With laws holy and divine, O Thesmophora you
    extend your hand.
Hail to you Demeter, Hail Europa, hail bull-eyed
    mother
May our praise of you echo through the world
    forever.

An Ecstatic Prayer to Ceres

by Christa A. Bergerson

For Valerie Wolfe

listen to her sing
from out of the emerald garden
listen to her voice ring

just between the crows' cacophony
and betwixt the towering cornrows
so deep beneath the verdant canopy
a wondrous Harvest Goddess sows

she offers this bountiful cornucopia
we shan't waste a piece of flesh, seed, nor vine
in spring, summer, and during Ambarvalia
these sacred fruits will bear us wine

we thank you for the harvest, so gold
we thank you for the food on our plates
we thank you for the blessings untold
we thank you for the varied tastes

oh mysterious Mother we offer you bull, sow, and
        sheep
may you shelter us through the darkened night
and keep the downtrodden and weary off their feet
we pray, bring us three seasons of love and light

Dear Ceres, Great Goddess, luminescent Mother of all
we will always adore you, we are willingly under your thrall

Demeter Invocation

by Romany Rivers

Belly of harvest
Walking the cornfields
Bringer of fruition
Teacher of the yield
Lover of the world
Mother of the grain
Wise woman of compromise
Wax and Wane
In you we feel
The wheel of the year
The season reflecting
Your laughter and tears
In joy we live in abundance
In grief we are bereft
The sun shines for your smile
Then only ice is left
Waiting in the barren
For the blessing of your womb
The gift of fertility
Returning from the tomb
Giving without end
Blessing scattered seed
Reaping in the harvest
Living without need
You are Queen of the lands
As far as eye can see

True Earth Mother
Wed unto the sea
Grant us your blessings
Make home our sacred space
Step into our Priestess
A Goddess with human face

Eleusis Bound

by Diotima Sophia

The travel through the stilled countryside
They return to Athens as to home
Crowds gather from far and wide —
Something said, something done, and something
 shown
The mysteries call again
To all they claim as their own
All classes of women and all of men
Something said, something done, and something
 shown.
The catechisms learned by rote
Recited, repeated, sometimes read
They must be voiced without aid of notes
Something shown, something done, and something
 said.
Ritual cleansing by the sea
Washing away lives previously led
Awake, arise, purified and free
Something shown, something done, and something
 said.
The mysteries of Demeter culminate
Far away from the blinding sun
From dark of sunset to Selene's full spate
Something shown, something said, and something
 done.
Thousands of voices — stilled in the night

The mysteries unfold, one on one
And not one to record the sight
Something shown, something said, and something
    done.

The Seed and the Fruit
by John Opsopaus

I. Theurgy

Theurgy is a very ancient practice, but the best documentation we have of it comes from the Neoplatonists, especially Iamblichus (c.245–c.325 CE) and Proclus (412–485 CE). It involves a number of operations intended to facilitate direct communication with the Gods. The most important operation is the *sustasis* (plural: *sustaseis*), which is a meeting, negotiation, and subsequent pact with a God or attendant spirit. This may be facilitated by another theurgical operation, *telestikê*, the animation or ensoulment of an icon, which "tunes" the image as an instrument for divine communication and divination.

In this chapter I will present and interpret two *sustaseis* with Demeter (conducted in 2000 and 2013), which will give, I hope, some insight into the meaning of the Eleusinian Mysteries in ancient times and for our time. It is natural and reasonable to be skeptical about such colloquies with the Gods. How can someone distinguish a genuine communication relevant to everyone from insights (or even fantasies!) peculiar to their reporter? Ultimately, we are all responsible for our own knowledge, and we must draw our own critical conclusions, even when reading the conclusions of eminent scientists and scholars. Therefore, especially in the case of theurgy, we must consider whether the report of a *sustasis* is consistent with our personal knowledge of a deity and with the reports of other theurgists and scholars. (Of course, you can conduct your own theurgical operations, as well.) Ultimately, you must decide if it rings true.

For the first theurgical operation (marked as "A" texts in the rest of this chapter), I closed my eyes and in my imagination descended by 55 steps the ten-level stairway into the Abaton of a temple. The number ten was chosen for Pythagorean reasons: it is a symbol of completeness, connecting unity at one level to unity at another (because $1+0 = 1$). Each deeper level was progressively longer, so I made one step (timed with the breath) on the first level, two on the next level down, and so on, making ten steps on the deepest level. (55 is the tenth triangular number: $55 = 1 + 2 + 3 + \ldots + 10$.)

For the second operation ("B" texts), conducted in 2013, I began by intoning Orphic Hymn #40 "To Eleusinian Demeter" (Athanassakis transl.). In my imagination I descended only eight steps into a ground-level cave-temple of Demeter. (Pythagoreans identify Rhea with Two and with its threefold power: Eight; see Liddell, Scott & Jones, s.v. Rhea) Opening my eyes, I invoked Demeter into an image, so this operation included animation. I invoked Her under the name "Deo" and asked Her what I should say about Her. I witnessed signs of successful animation including motion in the icon and sudden wind, breaking waves, and bursting sunlight (the operation was conducted out of doors).

II. The Daughter's Descent

In the first *sustasis* that I will describe, I invoked the Goddess to reveal to me the Logos Mystikos, the Holy Myth of Eleusis, not for curiosity, but for a planned group celebration of the Greater Mysteries. (I have explicit permission from the Goddess to present the material herein.)

> *The story starts with My father. Hades you call Him.*
> *He came to Me as a snake; We coupled, as I wished. (A1)*

This text implies that Hades is both the father and mate of Demeter, which is similar to the Orphic myths, but differs in several key respects. Orphic sources tell us that Zeus mated with Rhea, the Mother of the Gods (and His own mother) as snakes in a cave (West, pp. 73–4, 220). In some versions She gave birth to Demeter; in others She became Demeter (West, p. 217). We are also told that Zeus and Demeter mated as snakes, engendering Persephone, and that Zeus and Persephone mated as snakes, engendering Chthonic Dionysos (West, pp.

73–4, 220–1, 252). In the triad Rhea-Demeter-Persephone we really have three aspects of a Great Goddess (Crone-Mother-Maiden, if you like), for Rhea and Demeter are often identified in Orphism, and Demeter and Persephone are often identified in the Eleusinian Mysteries (West, pp. 93, 217; Kerényi, pp. 32–3). Here, however, it is not Zeus but Hades who mates with the Goddess. However, we will see that Zeus and Hades (often called "Chthonic Zeus") are often dual aspects of the God in the Mysteries (West, p. 95). Second, our traditional sources imply that Zeus pursued Rhea-Demeter-Persephone, who had changed Herself into a snake, and forced Himself on Her. Here, however, the Goddess asserts that this mating was Her intention, as we would expect from the Great Mother (see also B25–6 in Sec. XIII below).

The Goddess acknowledged the connection to the Orphic myth, and continued:

> *We came and coupled. There, beginning joined*
> *with end, and just as in the Ouroboros. (A2)*
> *Then I bore the daughter — Persephone.*
> *She too was destined for Hades. That's the cycle. (A3)*

Here She states explicitly the cycle of eternal life, which is the heart of the Eleusinian Mysteries. She presents the "rape" as follows:

> *Then She was placed upon the Rharian Plain,*
> *the field that's called the Plain of Dionysos,*
> *waiting for the Dark Lord to come.*
> *He came. He took Her away as prearranged.*
> *She knew this would happen, but she had to resist*
> *as we all do. It's part of life.*
> *She had to experience the reluctance to die.*
> *(A4)*

In the Homeric Hymn, Persephone is abducted from the Nysan Plain (*Nysion pedion*), which is associated with Mt. Nysa, where Dionysos (Dio-nysos) was born; the name is also associated with Dionysian cult sites (Kerényi, pp. 34–5). Here, however, the Goddess places the event on Rharian Plain, where the gift of agriculture was celebrated in the Mysteries (Kerényi, p. 127). She also makes clear that the Two Goddesses both understood the cosmic necessity of the Underworld Marriage. I remarked that the story of the daughter's resistance and reluctance to die — Her willing sacrifice — reminded me a little of Jesus, and Demeter replied:

> *The Christians stole the story from us for they knew a little of the Mysteries. (A5)*

The Mother proceeded to describe Her daughter's descent as follows:

> *And in this manner was She taken down,*
> *led by the Dark Prince, into the ground,*
> *the Chasm. And the pigs went with Her,*
> *sacrificed for the marriage feast.*
> *And Eubouleus — he saw them go,*
> *he who is himself the Dark Prince. (A6a)*

In the Hymn, Eubouleus is the swineherd whose pigs disappear underground with Hades and Persephone and who shows Demeter and Hekate the way into the Underworld (thus establishing the precedent for the pig sacrifice in the Thesmophoria, a festival for Demeter and Persephone). However, there is much more going on here, as the Goddess implies. "Eubouleus" means "He of Good Council" or "The Prudent One"; it is also an epithet of Zeus, Hades, Plouton (= Hades), Ploutos (Wealth), Child Dionysos, and perhaps Adonis (Kerényi, pp. 160–71). Perhaps we can interpret Eubouleus as a younger aspect of Hades, the Dark Prince. His name alludes also to the Boulê (council, decision, will) of Zeus

> to lure Persephone into a marriage which was so like death that all dying began with it, though through it life lost none

of its radiance but, on the contrary, was enriched. (Kerényi, p. 170)

Eubouleus leads the way to a better way of life, as revealed in the Mysteries (174).

> *In Her willing sacrifice She still cried out,*
> *and when Her mother — I — had heard it,*
> *She knew the deed was done.*
> *Just as I cried out when Dionysos took Me.*
> *(A6b)*

I think this is an important point: the sacrifice, though voluntary, is still traumatic. The mystical process of "dying before you die" is nevertheless a death. However, I do not understand the Goddess' reference to Dionysos taking Her, unless it is playing on the Parent-Child aspects (Demeter-Persephone / Zeus-Dionysos) and refers to Her mating with Zeus.

> *She went down to the Underworld to wed the Dark Lord.*
> *It all was prearranged. She veiled Herself.*
> *And later, on the wedding night,*
> *unveiled Herself to the initiates.*
> *For Dionysos was also an initiate into the mystery.*
> *Oh holy daughter, You have initiated us all!*
> *That is the true mystery! (A6c)*

An important part of the wedding ritual is the Unveiling (*anakaluptêria*), when the bride removes her maiden veil and reveals herself to her groom and the wedding party, and so also the Maiden would have unveiled Herself to the Unseen One and His host of shades. This text connects the Unveiling to the revelation or epiphany of the Goddess before the initiates at the climax of the Mysteries. It also states that Dionysos Himself was an initiate, perhaps as His alter ego, Eubouleus. (It might even refer to Hades in His youthful aspect, implying that the bride initiated the groom.) Finally, the Mother Goddess acknowledges that She Herself has been initiated by the Maiden, which is crucial for understanding the Mysteries, for the initiates imitate the Mother in Her quest for and recovery of Her child.

> *She, the Mediator, shows us all the way.*
> *She had to do it though We prearranged it.*
> *That was Her own destiny. (A7)*

As I understand it, the Father and Mother have arranged the Daughter's marriage to Death so that She can be a Mediator for us, arranging for initiates a better relationship to death and mortality; that is Her role in the divine bureaucracy. (Later, in A33–4, the Mother distinguishes Herself as Mediator from Her Daughter as Initiator, but in that context She is referring to Her mediation of Heaven and Earth.)

III. One and Many

I was quite confused by the various names and epithets that seemed to refer to the same Deities or to the same Deities in different aspects or generations, so I asked the Goddess for clarification.

> *These Deities are all the same.*
> *All manifestations of the All in different ways,*
> *splitting and recombining like clouds.*
> *We split so we can work against each other,*
> *create distinctions for the dynamism. (A8)*

In Neoplatonism, the Inexpressible One (*To Arrhêton Hen*) is the ultimate principle of unity beyond all duality, beyond Existence and Non-existence, beyond even Being and Non-being. As such, it is beyond verbal description or conceptualization, and can be known only through a theurgical processes of Union (*Henôsis*). The individual Gods are understood as articulations of this ineffable Unity, as Beings radiating from The One, unified by Sameness and distinguished by Difference (the Monad and the Indefinite Dyad, according to Pythagoreans). The Maiden made a similar point in my theurgical meetings with Her (Opsopaus 2012, secs. X, B1; XII, B3, B11). Here, however, the Mother tells a much more dynamic story, in which the Gods and Goddesses are continually forming new constellations of attributes and functions in order to govern the cosmos. Indeed, She points out that this differentiation of one God from another permits disagreement and strife among the Gods, which fuels the dynamism of existence (else everything would be a bland and static uniform plenum). As Heraclitus says, "opposition is fitting, and from differences comes the most beautiful harmony, and all things come to be through strife" (DK 22B8). Empedocles also understood that an organized cosmos requires two opposed forces: Love (*Philia*) and Strife (*Neikos*), the forces of union and separation. The Goddess explained Her own origin:

> *I come from the bisexual being,*
> *matter and spirit, joined in chaotic swirling darkness.*
> *Undifferentiated life: that*
> *is the beginning, that the Ur-mother.*
> *But this beginning was required to change,*
> *so the separation into dark and light,*
> *male and female, wet and dry, cool and hot,*
> *all these opposites, then came about.*
> *But they had to be rejoined again*
> *as the Ouroboros is rejoined. (A9)*

This is similar to Orphic cosmogonies, in which a bisexual God has an important role. For example, in the Orphic Rhapsodies the serpent Time encircles and squeezes the Cosmic Egg, which cracks (West, pp. 70, 86–7, 104–5, pp. 198–208). From it emerges bisexual Phanes ("the One Who Appears"), also called Protogonos (First Born). He mates with Himself and gives birth to Ouranos (Heaven) and Gê (Gaia, Earth). In myth and ritual, Gê and Demeter are often identified (Dêmêtêr is a dialectical variant of Gê-Mêtêr = Earth-Mother). Earth and Heaven may be compared with "matter and spirit" in our text. The Egg itself is created by Time in Aither and Chaos, which it also created (West, pp. 198–200, 230–1). Other cosmogonies, including the Orphic theogony of Eudemus, make Night the first principle, or Night and Air, as Epimenides taught (Kirk, Raven & Schofield, pp. 17–18). Aither, Air, Night, Chaos: they are similar to the "chaotic swirling darkness" mentioned here, which the Goddess identifies with undifferentiated Life and calls the Ur-mother. From this unity emerge all the opposites, including male and female, and the two pairs of opposed powers possessed by the elements (wet and dry, cool and hot). Empedocles also described a separation into opposites during the reign of Strife alternating cyclically with a reunification under the reign of Love. In Neoplatonism, we have the procession of The One into Multiplicity and Matter, and their return to The

One in an eternal (timeless) cycle (here symbolized by the Ouroboros Serpent).

Some days before my *sustasis* with the Goddess, I had an inspiration about the Mysteries, which I had written down:

> *This is the Secret:*
> *The One becomes Two,*
> *and the Two, by mediation of the Three,*
> *becomes One.*

(You may recognize this as a variation of the alchemical Axiom of Maria the Jewess.) My understanding was that The One divides into all these dualities (male-female, mother-daughter, father-son, etc.), but they are reunited by the mediation of the Goddess. I asked Demeter if my insight was correct.

> *Your version is a little too neat and schematic.*
> *It's all a continuous flow.*
> *We are the same and different at the same time.*
> *It's not sequential, all exist at once.*
> *That's the secret and the mystery.*
> *It's beyond all rational understanding. (A10)*

So we must avoid slipping into a temporal picture of emanation, or of cyclic procession and return. The theogony is timeless. I asked Her if this ineffable mystery was like The Inexpressible One of the Platonists.

> *They left out matter. That's part of the All too.*
> *That's part of the mystery at Eleusis. (A11)*

I interpret this to mean that the physical embodiment of life is essential to the Eleusinian Mysteries. I asked Her who understood the Mysteries, and whom I could read.

> *Psellos knows some, and Kerényi; they are good.*
> *Aristotle knew some, also Plutarch.*
> *But you need to reconstruct it since*
> *no one of them ever wrote it down*
> *(in anything that you can get).*
> *So continue reading and talking to Me. (A12)*
> *Your mysteries will evolve like the ancient ones.*
> *The first enactments will be good for a start. (A13)*

IV. Hierosgamos

The Goddess continued Her narration of the Sacred Myth:

> *They're married and go to the marriage bed.*
> *Aphrodite does this; Eros helps. (A14)*

To be sure I understood, I asked if She meant that Persephone and Dionysos/Hades went to the bed. She clarified:

> *Hades is a place, and Dionysos the God.*
> *Hades is the unseen place, the unconscious.*
> *(A15)*

"Hades" (Grk. Haidês) is derived from *aidês*, which means "unseen." By equating it to the unconscious, She has moved to a more psychological explanation of the Mysteries. Eros enables the union in the unconscious:

> *That is where the marriage must take place*
> *and where all such marriages take place.*
> *(A16)*
> *It is a rejoining of the disjoined parts*
> *(as Jung saw).*
> *We each must do it, as initiates.*
> *The vision helps the process, as a catalyst.*
> *(A17)*

Here She has moved from the process of psychological integration (which Jung called individuation, from Latin *individuus*, which means "undivided") to the psycho-integrative effect of the epiphany of the Maiden at the climax of the Mysteries. I asked how such an epiphany might be achieved today.

> *Bring it to pass by trance and invitation.*
> *If you are sincere, then I will help,*
> *but you all must be sincere.*
> *Then it will come to each — or not — as they need.*
> *That is the way it works — for you too.*
> *(A18)*

There are two important points here. First, an epiphany of a Goddess is not something that can be engineered; rather it is granted as a gift. Second, it is granted as a function of need; some people might not need it at a particular time or ever.

The Goddess continued Her narration of the Eleusinian Myth:

> *The Goddess returns and gives birth from the fire. (A20)*

This alludes to the great eruption of light and fire at the climax of the Mysteries in which the Daughter appears. I mentioned to the Goddess that Carl Kerényi (pp. 101–2) associates the Maiden with fire, and the Goddess said that both he and Peter Kingsley are correct, which confused me, since Kingsley argues that Empedocles associates Her with Water, which is significant for understanding Her as the Lady of Dissolution (Opsopaus 2012, Sec. V). She replied:

> *Both correspondences can be correct,*
> *for She is paradoxical.*
> *The opposites are joined in the Underworld.*
> *Recall the Fire and Water in the rivers.*
> *(A21)*

The rivers in the underworld are fiery, thus combining the opposites Water and Fire (Kingsley, pp. 73–4, 96–102). However, each of the four rivers is associated with an element, and in a *sustasis* with the Maiden, She said that She sits beside the Pyriphlegethon (the River of Fire) with Hekate, who is associated with Fire (Opsopaus 2012, sec. XIII). She said, "We are Fire and Water. / So we are the Opposites who are not opposites" (Opsopaus 2012, A17) which reflects the paradoxical obscurity of the Underworld.

> *She brings the Water to the Fire of Hades.*
> *But Dionysos also is Water,*
> *and She brings the Fire to Him.*
> *Dionysos is like Zeus.*
> *The opposites are joined in the marriage.*
> *(A22)*

Hades is also associated with Fire because He is ruler of the Central Fire, as argued by Kingsley (pp. 47–53, 71–8). Water is associated with Dionysos because He is Lord of Moist Nature (Otto, ch. 14), that is, moist green vegetation, and of Wine (liquid spirits, "fire water"). Likewise Zeus is the God who brings the fertilizing rain, who is invoked on the Rharian Plain to fertilize Earth. However, in my *sustaseis* with the Maiden, She associated both Dionysos and Zeus with Air (Opsopaus 2012, secs. II, VII). (Kingsley argues that Empedocles also associates Zeus with Air, in which the dominant quality is moistness.) However, these associations have more to do with the alchemical Rotation of the Elements. The significance of the symbolism of the conjunction of opposites in the Underworld is that initiation is achieved though this unification:

> *So also all the opposites must be rejoined,*
> *rejoined in all initiates.*
> *By joining them all, the initiate enters*
> *into a unitary state with the All. (A23)*

I asked Her if She was referring to the Neoplatonic Union (*Henōsis*) with the ineffable and paradoxical One:

> *It is the same as the mysteries, but done individually. (A24)*

That is, the Neoplatonic practice of *Henôsis* is a solitary exercise, whereas the Mysteries achieved a kind of collective experience of union.

V. Flow and Blood

I began to ask the Mother Goddess to tell me more of Her Mysteries, but She interrupted me:

Correction! My daughter's Mysteries! (A25)

That is, Persephone has created the Mysteries, and Demeter merely provides the model for all initiates. The Goddess continued:

The story is about the grain too,
the seed, the sperma, the form-giving element.
The seed goes through the process too. (A26a)

In Ancient Greek, *sperma* means seed, specifically the seed of plants, but more generally the sperm of animals (Liddell, Scott & Jones, s.v.). Metaphorically, *sperma* refers to the origin and species of a living thing, its form. The Goddess tells us that seed goes through the initiation process: it is put in the Earth, where it rots, which breaks down its rigid shell, but then it sprouts, drawing sustenance from Earth, to manifest new life above ground. The form of life comes from the seed; its substance is from Earth.

> *The essence of life is in plant life: Zôê.*
> *You must learn to reconnect with plant life.*
> *That's where immortality's achieved.*
> *Immortality will flow through you.*
> *You are the vessel. That is how*
> *immortality is achieved by you.*
> *You must come to know this. (A26b)*

Ancient Greek has two words for "life": *zôê* and *bios*. The feminine noun *zôê* has more the sense of the force of life itself and of existence in the universe; it is related to a verb *zô*, meaning "to live." Masculine *bios*, in contrast, refers to a manner of living, or to a specific life; we may speak of your *bios* or my *bios*; it is related to the verb *biô*, meaning "to pass one's life." Here the Goddess tells us that immortality is a matter of the Life Force flowing through everyone rather than of the continuity of individual life. I think that what we are supposed to discover — experientially — in the Mysteries is that just as each seed of grain has its individual life, but Grain lives forever, so also are our individual lives in relation to Human Life. The Goddess confirms this interpretation as follows:

> *Forget ego! That is the mistake.*
> *That's what you must learn in the Mysteries.*

> *The Life Force flows through you. It's never-ending,*
> *but your ego is just a temporary vessel.*
> *That is what you must see in the Vision.*
> *(A26c)*

That is, our individual egos or personalities do not achieve immortality; they perish like individual grain sprouts. Rather, we are the husks or vessels through which the immortal Life Force ever flows. We overvalue our egos and imagine there is some great value in the survival of our individual personalities and memories.

In the last line above, the Goddess says that this lesson is what we learn in the Vision that is the climax of the Mysteries in the Telesterion. Kerényi (p. 94) speculates that the head of the Maiden appeared in the midst of the enormous fire. I asked the Goddess if we experience Eternal Life in the head of Korê (the Maiden).

> *Not in the head of Korê;*
> *in the flow, the infinite roaring flow.*
> *Remember Rhea.*
> *She is both the Flow and Pomegranate.*
> *(A27a)*

The image is in the roaring fire from the Underworld, which continues to exist so long as there is fuel for the flame. She connects this eternal flux of Life with Rhea (Rhea, Rheê), whose name was connected both with "flow" (*rheô* = to flow; *rhoê, rhoá* = river, flowing, flux) and with "pomegranate" (*rhóa*), differing only in a shift in accent.

> *She is the Húês too. Flow and blood.*
> *When the blood flows, there is life.*
> *That is the meaning of the blood*
> *flowing on the ground creating life.*
> *It's the spirit becoming embodied in matter.*
> *(A27b)*

Húês is an epithet of both Zeus and Dionysos as Gods of the Fertilizing Rain (which also reinforces Their association with Water). It comes from the verb *huô*, which means "to rain." In the aftermath of the Eleusinian Mysteries, the initiates went into the Rharian Field, where they repeatedly invoked *Hue! Kue!* (Rain! Conceive!). It was called the Mystical Formula (*Rhêsis Mystikê*), and the Neoplatonist Proclus reports that the priest looked to the Heavens when calling the first word and toward the Earth when calling the second (Kerényi, p. 141). In this way the Sky Father and Earth Mother ensure the continuation of corporeal Life (spirit embodied in matter).

However, this passage refers to blood, not rain, and I wondered where the flowing of blood on the ground occurs in the Eleusinian Myth, and She replied:

> *It doesn't.*
> *It's in the story of Dionysos as the Child,*
> *which follows on the Mysteries,*
> *but also comes in a form with Korê's death*
> *and shedding Hymenal blood, the blood of marriage.*
> *As virgins are deflowered on the stone in Rome,*
> *she sheds her Hymenal blood on the Omphalos,*
> *itself, a vehicle of the spirit,*
> *from the mother to the child,*
> *from earth to heaven and vice versa. (A28)*

The Goddess has used fertilizing blood flowing on the Earth to make a connection with the Orphic myth of Dionysos: how He was torn apart by the Titans, who were then incinerated by Zeus's lightning bolt. Humans were created from the ash, which combines divine Olympic and earthly Titanic elements. Blood flowing in the Earth, as a symbol of death and rebirth (cf. also the myths of Attis and Adonis) is then connected with the hymenal blood shed by the Daughter after Her descent into the Underworld. This seems to be mentioned as a precedent for the practice in Rome by which betrothed maidens deflowered themselves on a sacred stone, here called an Omphalos (navel stone). The Omphalos is described as a vehicle of the spirit, by which it is transmitted from the mother to the fetus; blood established the connection. By extension, the Cosmic Omphalos is the channel by which spirit descends from Heaven to Earth and ascends again from Earth back to Heaven. To be sure, I asked whether the flux was from Heaven to Earth or Earth to Heaven. She said:

> *Both.*
> *Remember the fire and water in the Hierosgamos.*
> *This is another mystery.*
> *They are both masculine and feminine.*
> *Don't worry too much about the genders.*
> *(A29)*

The *Hierosgamos* (sacred wedding) is between the opposites, Fire and Water. Traditionally Fire is masculine and Water is feminine, and this could be the union of Hades and Persephone (Opsopaus 2012). However, Dionysos, who is a youthful double of Hades, is associated with Water and the fertilizing fluid, as is Zeus. So it is unclear who is bride and who is groom in the *Hierosgamos*, and I think the Goddess is warning us not to be too concerned about the genders. The mystery, as She will explain, is that the Child is reborn from a Union of Opposites (*Coniunctio Oppositorum*).

VI. The Child Reborn

The Goddess continues the Sacred Myth:

The Child returns, reborn, restarts the story.
That's the essence of the Ouroboros Cycle.
(You are too concerned with making it a story.) (A30)

The rebirth of the Divine Child (whether Dionysos or Persephone) starts a new cycle. This is the Ouroboros Cycle: the Cosmic Serpent consuming itself, fertilizing and giving birth to Itself, which the Goddess alluded to earlier in Her narration (A2, A9). She chides me for falling into the error of thinking of the Myth as a linear story rather than an eternal cycle. She continues:

The child, like all initiates, is reborn from fire.
That's what initiation means.
He sees the light of day for the first time like a baby.
Earth hands Him to Me, and I nurture Him.
So I, a nurturing mother, care for all initiates,
as I tried to care for young Demóphoön.
(A31)

The Maiden is reborn through Her union with Hades, ruler of the Central Fire, and is led up out of the Earth by Hekate, also associated with Fire (Opsopaus 1998, "Fire"). Likewise, Dionysos is reborn in fire when Semele (also called Huê) is incinerated by Zeus's fiery brilliance. The Fire brings about the illumination of the Reborn One. (See Opsopaus 2012 for the Alchemical Rotation: Earth through Fire leading to rebirth in Air.) As initiates, we follow the lead of the Mother, and She cares for us as spiritual newborns. I asked Her the meaning of the Demophoön episode.

> *It shows how foolishness aborts the process.*
> *It shows the necessity of surrender —*
> *both the initiate-child's and the mother's.*
> *We must let go of the old. That is the lesson.*
> *We must die to it to earn new life.*
> *Korê's death was painful, but chosen willingly.*
> *Christ's too, who knew the initiation process,*
> *but he didn't know the fire and water. (A32)*

I think this passage speaks for itself. The Christian version is lopsided, unbalanced, for it doesn't unify the opposites.

VII. Initiator and Mediator

As I reached the limits of my ability to sustain the *sustasis*, I asked the Goddess what else was important to say about the Eleusinian Mysteries.

> *Only this.*
> *The Daughter must return, which is Her destiny,*
> *part of the cycle. She is the cycle,*
> *a wheel — yes — but a wheel in life,*
> *everlasting life. The vision shows the wheel.*
> *Like a flock of birds, the vision is of life en masse. (A33a)*

That is, the Daughter teaches us the universal cycle of life, not just the agricultural cycle, which is only one aspect of the greater cycle. A flock of birds illustrates the idea in that it has a life and behavior of its own, largely independent of the individual birds in the flock, who may move within the flock, take the lead or be a follower, or even die and leave the flock, which goes on without them. Eternal life continues, independent of individual births and deaths, but sustained by them.

> *Ask My Daughter for the vision.*
> *Open to Her and She will give it.*
> *She is the Initiator.*
> *I am just the Mediator. (A33b)*

We follow the path of the Mother in order to be initiated by the Daughter. I expressed surprise at Her statement, since being a mediator seemed too small a role for Demeter, an Earth Goddess, but She explained that Her mediation is alchemical:

> *The Earth must be a Mediator, both*
> *between the fire and water, and*
> *between the Heavens and the Underworld.*
> *(A34a)*

Earth mediates between fire and water because it is cool and dry; it has dryness in common with fire, which is warm and dry, and coolness in common with water, which is cool and moist. But Earth also resides between the Heavens above and the Underworld below. The Mother says of Her Daughter:

> *She is the Ghost, the Spirit, that must live inside.*
> *Let Her come. I will show the way,*
> *open the way, allowing Her to meet you.*
> *You must both move, both meet in the middle,*
> *in the fire and the water.*
> *That is what you must do.*
> *That is what we did after Hekáte*
> *showed the way; we met in the middle.*
> *(A34b)*

As Queen of the Underworld, She may be called a ghost, but a ghost who lives within the world, but also perhaps in us. The Mother shows us the way to the Maiden, who ascends from the Underworld to reveal the Mystery to us. The reunion of the Mother and the Daughter was arranged by torch-bearing Hekate, and Hermes, the preeminent boundary-crosser, Psychopomp, guide of souls to the Nether Regions, is there, too. However, as fire symbolizes Hekate, perhaps water symbolizes Dionysos, for the Goddess continues:

> *Dionysos stays behind; He comes another time.*
> *That is another mystery. Listen!*
> *Each God must come in His own time. That is the rule.*
> *Invite each when it is time. Don't rush it.*
> *Now is the time for Persephone and for Me.*
> *It is right. Now is the time for Matter —*
> *Mêtêr — it is overdue.*
> *We will do this, bring it about.*
> *That is all for now. I wish you well. (A34c)*

This seems very important to me: each age has needs for particular Gods and Goddesses. While Dionysos must be honored as a God, and deserves our devotion, our relation with the Two Goddesses is more relevant now. This relevance is grounded in the importance of matter (derived from Mêtêr, Mother), that is, in the immanent divinity of Nature. I explore this in Section IX below.

This completed the first *sustasis* with the Goddess.

VIII. Living on Earth

In a second theurgical operation the Goddess began by focusing on environmental issues. When I asked what I should write about, She replied:

> *You should focus on the Earth — the climate.*
> *That is most important, for I am Gaia too.*
> *I live in Her, beneath the soil.*
> *This is My realm, and My daughter's too.*
> *This you know. (B1–2)*

The Goddess explicitly identifies Herself with Gaia, which was implicit in the previous *sustasis* (A34a in Sec. VII above). I asked if She had an environmental message, and She answered:

> *The crops will fail unless the environment is fixed. I'm suffocating. This must be fixed.*
> *Too much air — of the wrong kind — can kill.*
> *But you know all of this. (B6)*

By "air of the wrong kind" I assume She means pollution or greenhouse gasses. I asked if there is a spiritual aspect to our environmental problems.

> *Is there a spiritual part? There always is!*
> *For you must do the practices: restraint [in all things].*
> *And this is the beginning. Spread the word.*
> *(B7)*

Most of the ancient philosophies taught some form of restraint and simple living (e.g., Stoicism and Epicureanism). However, I objected that people in our culture will not listen, and in any case the message of restraint has been preached for many years.

> *The message of restraint was often pitched,*
> *but now it's different. Now it's critical. (B8)*
> *Now the life of Earth itself's at stake.*
> *Now it all just might collapse, and not*
> *just humans. (B9)*

I asked how this was possible, and She replied:

> *[Collapse] by poisoning of everything. (B10)*

I continued to express concern that writing about this would just sound like an environmental rant, and asked Her about the spiritual perspective.

> *People must talk to Me to learn My ways.*
> *My ways are green, for sure, but they are also*
> *deeply spiritual, and about rebirth. (B11)*

This is an argument for theurgic communication with Demeter in general, but more specifically about the Eleusinian Mysteries, which are explored in the following sections.

IX. Alchemical Rebirth

I asked the Goddess what to say about the Mysteries of the Mother and Daughter.

> *Rebirth is the key.*
> *Rebirth of the Earth as well.*
> *For that is how all humans will survive.*
> *I taught the secrets at Eleusis. (B3)*

That is, the Eleusinian Mysteries were concerned with the rebirth of the Earth, not just the rebirth of individuals, discussed above. I asked about the secrets and whether it would be permissible to tell them.

Not all of them.
I will tell you what you need to know.
For it's about environment and crops.
For that is what you all now need to know.
(B4a)

That is, I think, the relevant information has to do with the agricultural cycle and the turning of the seasons (the most superficial meaning of the Eleusinian Mysteries).

The crops — they are My children — the father is
Triptolemos: a secret you can tell.
We're in the field, and we give birth to crops.
For also We are Iason and Myself. (B4b)

In the Homeric Hymn, after the Daughter is returned to the Mother, and They are reconciled to the New Order, Demeter teaches Her rites and mysteries to Triptolemos, who made them available to all mortals. His name means Triple-warrior (Kerényi, p. 126; see also Sec. X below). She goes on to identify him with Iason (Iasion), with whom She mated in the thrice-plowed field, according to Cretan myth, for He is the Great Hunter Zagreus, the Dark Lord who captures all mortals just as He seized the Maiden (Kerényi, p. 30). This suggests a union between the Earth Goddess and this Threefold Power.

> *We are the two who bring this all to pass —*
> *alchemically. The birth of spirit — of life —*
> *in matter, and materialized spirit too.*
> *The Seed — the alchemical Egg — embodies this.*
> *It is the Vessel of Birth.*
> *This is what I showed in the Mysteries. (B4c)*

The union of the Mother and the Dark Lord is a union of spirit or life with dark primordial matter, that is, spirit materialized (embodied) and matter spiritualized (animated), which is the alchemical *Coniunctio Oppositorum*. This mystical union takes place in the Alchemical Egg, which is the Seed, both literally and figuratively.

> *My daughter showed these Mysteries with me,*
> *for She is Soror Mystica as well.*
> *We are both one, and two sides of the coin;*
> *and as you know Hekáte makes the third.*
> *She does the Magic making it all work.*
> *For She's the Artificer! That's Her role.*
> *What more? (B4d)*

The *Soror Mystica* is the female partner of the male Alchemist. The Great Work cannot be accomplished without their close collaboration, and their union on the physical level mirrors and foreshadows the union on the spiritual level of the complementary Elements or Principles. By calling Her Artificer and connecting Her with Magic, Demeter reminds us that Hekate is a Witch, whose magic enables the alchemical operation. The Daughter, Mother, and Witch (or Crone) are a trinity.

I asked the Goddess what people should do with this information.

> *They can have a practice of their own:*
> *to do themselves the alchemy of Nature,*
> *see the spirit hid in matter and*
> *materialize the spirit, for this means*
> *that all is living and must be seen this way.*
> *(B5)*

I asked Her to be more specific, and She offered this exercise (see also Sec. XII):

> *Get down to the earth. Look at it. Smell it.*
> *See its life. It's the living flesh,*
> *which holds the Seed, the Vessel. Come to know it.*
> *It may be dry, but it's the Root of Growth,*
> *the Medium, the Matrix, the Womb of Birth,*
> *beginning small but then becoming large.*

> *It's My Rule, My Way.*
> *This is the process of growth, and I am Growth.*
> *This is My name too. (B13)*

We have already seen the Seed as the Alchemical Egg (B4c), and will learn more of it in Section X. Here the focus is on the soil, which nurtures the rebirth taking place in the seed. Since She called Herself "Growth," I asked if She meant that She is *Φύσις (Phusis)*, which is the ancient Greek word for Nature, but comes from a root (*phuô*) that means to produce, to beget, to cause to grow. She answered:

> *Φύσις too: Growth and Nature. (B14)*

Are You above us as the World Soul, I asked Her, or Nature here, or below the Earth?

> *I am everywhere: above, below, and here.*
> *I am Growth wherever it takes place.*
> *For that's My Nature and My Name. (B15)*

That is, She is a Threefold Power of Growth, ruling in the Three Realms, like Hekate.

X. Seed and Fruit

I asked the Goddess how to explain the Seed.

The Seed is My teachings, My teachings about rebirth.
They are the Key, the Key to the Kingdom.
This is what you must say to them:
The wisdom of rebirth — of renewal —
environmental as well as personal.
Call upon them to become
green inside, become organic,
to become integral and functional,
assist the whole in its survival.
This is the Key — to survival. And thriving.
(B12)

To rephrase, the key to both environmental and personal renewal is the teaching of the Goddess; this is the vessel by which we may be reborn more integrated and whole. We must become as the green, living kernel within the seed's shell, so that through our individual rebirth we may facilitate cultural and environmental renewal.

I asked the Goddess to relate Her teachings back to the Eleusinian Mysteries.

My daughter is Rebirth. She is the means
of rebirth and She is the instrument.
She's also Rebirth itself. She shows the Way.

> *As She goes, so may each of you go too.*
> *(B16a)*

In one sense, the Mother shows the way, by Her seeking of the Maiden, but in another way, the Daughter is the model for us, for She descends into the Underworld and becomes the Bride of Death. She undergoes the alchemical rotation (Opsopaus 2012).

> *Then follow Her upon the Path to Hades.*
> *Partake the Pomegranate. Then return.*
> *For Putrefaction must precede Rebirth.*
> *This is my lesson. I give birth to Her,*
> *but She must go the Way, and do the Process.*
> *That's the way with all things that are born.*
> *(B16b)*

One way of partaking the pomegranate is described in Section XII below. Putrefaction is the first stage in the alchemical *Magnum Opus*, for things must be reduced to Prime Matter before they can be reconstituted in a better form (to create the *Lapis Philosophorum*). (See Opsopaus 2012 for Persephone as the Lady of Dissolution.)

> *You too. For you have birth from Me; My daughter*
> *leads the Way, away from the world of life,*

> *to the World of Eternity and Shades,*
> *but then She leads you back into this world.*
> *(B16c)*

The Daughter makes this journey between the worlds, and by Her grace, we can too. What is the objective?

> *There are Fruits — for you — for everyone.*
> *That's what my gift of agriculture means.*
> *Triptolemos is still the Child with Three*
> *Powers who can bring this to fruition.*
> *(B16d)*
> *They're Life and Power and Intelligence.*
> *(B17)*

Although these three are reminiscent of the Life-Being-Intellect triad of Neoplatonism, during the *sustasis* they reminded me of Plato's tripartite soul, which might be interpreted as Life (the appetitive soul), Will (the spirited soul), and Intelligence (the rational soul), so I asked Her if by "Power" She meant Will.

> *Will's part of it, but also the Potential*
> *to be all things. Unmanifest Potential.*
> *The Medium. Infinite Flexibility. The Malleable.*
> *The Medium of Life and Intellect,*

> *which give it Form. It is the Will to be changed —*
> *to allow your self to be formed, to be informed,*
> *to be transformed — by what's outside of you.*
> *Humility to be the Form of Higher*
> *Powers that work through you. Thus you must*
> *become an agent of the Goddess — of Me.*
> *For know that you're all subject to the Earth —*
> *that is your Nature — born of Titanic Ash.*
> *That is your Destiny. You're the Dionysos —*
> *the Son of God — continually reborn.*
> *That's human nature; you must actualize it,*
> *make it real, fulfill your destiny.*
> *It's what the Mysteries teach, and show the Way. (B18)*

It is clear from the foregoing that by "Power" the Goddess means something akin to Latin *Poetentia* and Greek *Dunamis*: that is, Potential, and in particular the infinite potential to be anything, as determined by Life and Intellect. This is Will in the sense that it is the willingness and also the intention to manifest the forms bestowed by Life and Intellect. She translates this from the metaphysical level to the personal level by saying that it is the humility to be an agent of the Gods, and in particular, of Her.

This is indeed one of the powers of Triptolemos, for he was a willing agent of the Goddess, promulgating Her Mysteries. This is no weakness, but the power of realizing whatever is required by the Gods. As the Goddess explains, we are all semidivine, born of the Titans but also of the Gods. As Earth Goddess, She rules us through the Titanic Ash — the matter — of which we're made. But, like Dionysos, we're also descended from the Olympian Gods, and by living willingly our dual nature we fulfill our destinies.

XI. Contemplation

I asked the Goddess what we should do in this age, when we no longer have the Eleusinian Mysteries.

> *The Mysteries can be created anew, but that is a conversation for another time. (B19)*
> *Here is what you all must do:*
> *Study the Mysteries. Study My Myth. (B20)*

I asked if She meant the Homeric Hymn to Demeter.

> *The Homeric Hymn and other versions.*
> *See the hidden thread. For you will know it better*
> *if you see it rather than if I tell it.*

This is a prescription for rebirth,
but do not follow it too literally.
Don't act it out. It's not a play.
That's not the best way. It's interior.
The Way of the Gods. (B21a)
Read Homer and Hesiod: that is primary.
Homer and Hesiod knew the Mysteries.
Wait,
and insight will come. That is enough for now. (B27)

To paraphrase, we should learn Her Mysteries by reading the ancient sources: Hesiod, Homer, and especially the Homeric Hymn to Demeter. But we should not read these literally, and instead seek the hidden prescription for rebirth. A dramatic reenactment of the myth is not what's called for. Rather, we should seek a series of introspective, contemplative exercises based on the Myth and the Mystery. I think She is also telling us to be humble, and to be willing to wait for inspiration from the Goddess, which She will grant us when it fits Her purposes.

XII. The Pomegranate Ritual

The Goddess offered this specific ritual:

Do this: Take a pomegranate. Eat it.
Imagine eating each seed as a life.

> *You're stocking up these many lives from Earth.*
> *Repeat My name with each one that you eat.*
> *Then think of Me and of My daughter too,*
> *of the Eternal Bond between Us twain,*
> *the Bond that never breaks. The Seed and the Fruit. (B21a)*

As She said this I received an image of the two ends of a dumbbell shape.

> *We alternate, and that's the Mystery.*
> *We alternate in power, as you can too.*
> *Above and below, living and dying. (B21b)*

That is, as the Mother and Daughter are complements, and as They each mate their opposites, so we alternate between living while we live and dying before we die, alternately above the earth and below it, fully conscious in each state. The ritual continues:

> *When it's eaten, contemplate Our Mystery.*
> *Replay the Myth in your mind. Take each part.*
> *Be sure to feel yourself as each of Us.*
> *Not just Me and My daughter. Be Hekáte*
> *too, and Hades, and the Sun, and Zeus,*
> *but most especially be ye Dionysos,*
> *as He is born of Chthonic Zeus and of*

> *My daughter, only to be born again,*
> *many times. This will be you as well. (B22)*

In other words, after eating the pomegranate has transported you to a contemplative state, visualize the Eleusinian Myth, imagining yourself as one or the other of the characters, for they all have important roles to play. In this way you will get at its essence from all these sides. However, She has told us a key fact: the role of Dionysos is the most important one for us.

XIII. Darkness

I asked the Goddess if She were referring to reincarnation at the end of B22 (Sec. XII).

> *This is a notion of reincarnation — true! —*
> *but not as you conceive it — very different!*
> *Your idea is much too egotistic.*
> *The ego does not need to be reborn.*
> *The ego is ephemeral — as it should be —*
> *of a day — for it's a Creature of Light.*
> *(B23a)*

This will be a hard idea for many reincarnationists to accept: the ego is not reincarnated; it does not survive. In the end, all our individual memories, thoughts, and personality traits are of little importance, though we cling to them as our essence, what defines us as individuals. But they are *Bios* not *Zôê* (recall Sec. V), and only *Zôê*, the Life Force, is eternal; this is our eternal life, our immortality. Our egos are ephemeral, which literally means "of a day" (*epi hêmera*).

> *But learn: the Seed's a Creature of the Dark.*
> *The Seed must germinate within the Dark.*
> *It later seeks the Light, but only when*
> *the alchemy is done, and then it seeks*
> *new Form, in order to be fruitful too.*
> *Be fruitful now, I say, but be prepared*
> *to give that up and rot within the Earth.*
> *(B23b)*

I understand this to mean that the inmost kernel of the Life Force (the "Highest Flower of the Soul" in Neoplatonism, the "Golden Flower" of Chinese alchemy) must develop outside of the light of consciousness, hidden in the alchemical vessel, whence it will emerge transformed, the life-enhancing Stone of the Wise. But the first stage of alchemical transformation is putrefaction, the reduction to unformed matter, pure potentiality, and so She says that after we live upon the earth, we must rot within it. I asked Her if She were saying we should be buried rather than cremated.

> *That doesn't matter. You're being too literal.*

The Earth — My Element — is cool and moist.
It's nurturing. All things may transform in the Dark,
and in this Darkness is My Magic done.
Within the Dark all things dissolve, which means
they can re-form into a newer form —
a transformation, self-transcending change.
This is My Way: a germination in
the Earth, so you are able to ascend. (B24)

Traditionally, of course, the element Earth is cool and dry, so I think She is making a different point: that the Underworld is the realm of cool dissolution, of loss of form, which is the effect of the moist power (Opsopaus 2012, secs. III, V) and the precondition for the growth of new form. Obviously the seed germinates under the earth in the dark, but more importantly the dark Underworld is the place where magical and alchemical transformations can take place (Opsopaus 2012, sec. IX). The Dark-robed Goddess and the Unseen God reign there. I remarked that Her account was poetic, but not too specific.

Specific! That is all you ever want!
You must let the poetry sink in.
Read and contemplate. And memorize
some parts if you would learn the Mysteries.

> *For they cannot be told, but only lived!*
> *For this is My Realm — the living Mystery.*
> *(B25a)*

Here the Goddess expands on the practice that She described in B22 (Sec. XII above). We are to read, and reread, and remember the myths relevant to to the Eleusinian Mysteries, and in our contemplations we are to imagine ourselves in the roles of the various protagonists. By living the myths in our minds, we will come to understand them. She continued:

> *Indeed, this Mystery of Mine is why*
> *I gave My daughter to the Underworld.*
> *(B25b)*

To be sure I understood, I asked Her if She willed Her daughter's descent.

> *Of course I willed it, for it had to be!*
> *My daughter and I are one — two sides, two aspects.*
> *I waited for Zeus in the Cave, became a Snake,*
> *and He transformed into a Snake as well:*
> *underworld souls that in the Underworld mate*
> *engendering in mysterious ways a Child,*
> *whether Persephone or Dionysos —*

Daughter or Son — it doesn't really matter;
We are all the same beneath the Symbols.
Our Names are Our Functions.
We have many things to do in this world.
(B26)

Thus it seems that the underworld Mother and Father — Demeter and Zeus Chthonios — mate and give birth to the alchemical Child, either (or both) Persephone and Chthonic Dionysos. As She explained previously (A8, A10, Sec. III), the Gods emerge variously from The Ineffable One in order to accomplish Their various purposes, in this case to show us the way to eternal life by means of the Eleusinian Mysteries.

Bibliography

Athanassakis, Apostolos N., and Wolkow, Benjamin M. (2013). *The Orphic Hymns: Translation, Introduction, and Notes.* Johns Hopkins Univ. Press.

Kerényi, Carl (1967). *Eleusis: Archetypal Image of Mother and Daughter,* tr. Ralph Manheim. Princeton Univ. Press.

Kingsley, Peter. (1995). *Ancient Philosophy, Mystery and Magic: Empedocles and Pythagorean Tradition.* Oxford University Press.

Kirk, G. S., Raven, J. E., and Schofield, M. (1983). *The Presocratic Philosophers*, 2nd ed. Cambridge Univ. Press.

Liddell, H. G., Scott, R., & Jones, H. S. (1968). *A Greek-English Lexicon, With a Supplement*, 1968, 9th ed. Oxford: Oxford University Press.

Opsopaus, John (1998). "The Ancient Greek Esoteric Doctrine of the Elements." http://omphalos.org/BA/AGEDE

Opsopaus, John (2012). "Meetings with the Maiden," in Melitta Benu (Ed.), *Queen of the Sacred Way: A Devotional Anthology in Honor of Persephone* (pp. 190–220). Neos Alexandria.

Otto, Walter (1965). *Dionysus: Myth and Cult*, tr. R. B. Palmer. Bloomington: Indiana Univ. Press.

West, Martin L. (1983). *The Orphic Poems*. Oxford Univ. Press.

Eleusinia Goetia

by P. Sufenas Virius Lupus

He was not expecting the sounds to come from the depths,
even though he knew the clang of cymbal and tambor
from the Phrygian priests of the Great Mother.

He had heard the lament for Palaimon in Corinth,
and had recalled the women's cries for Adonis
on many a humid summer evening in his youth.

But this was a different sort of weeping,
a lamenting and a crying that shook the sinews
of his soul near clear of bodily fetters.

It was painful in the depths of his marrows to hear
the wail welling up from the depths of the telestrion,
the howl more plaintive than the howl of all the
wolves of Arcadia.

The chains of Chronos melted around him
revealing a titanic gap in the cosmos,
empty, filled only with the wail of the Mother.

The daughter, the Maiden, lost to her embraces,
and even more heart-rending, more bowel-churning,
more tear-deluging, the child in the fire on the floor.

A thousand images flashed before him, the
	Bithynian boy,
of the goddess of olives and spear-points
who had never yet had a brother born to her ...

Of the Queen of the Gods and her brother and step-
	daughter
swayed from rebellion by the gentle arms
of a titaness who called the sea her realm ...

And of that titaness, married off to a mortal
so that a child by the Earth-Shaker or Thunderer
would not upset the order of the cosmos ...

And even the child of her daughter by her brother,
father of the daughter himself, who in a mirror's
	flash
would lose the kingship of the gods for a time.

But one would yet come who might be all of these,
or perhaps two or more — for who could say?
The shadows of lives yet unlived were an
	oppressive tumult.

Out of them, he saw a young man near him, a few
	years older,
now decades older, a husband and father and
	consul,
with his child initiated at the hearth, happy ...

And the wife, called by the name of the goddess
    Deo,
near him and alive, but then dying suddenly,
only to be the image of the goddess and in her
    company …

A child, older than Demophoön but not as old as he,
in the chlamys of the ephebes, being instructed
as his ship sailed for the cold spring past the white
    tree …

With a rush, he became dizzy, his stomach like an
    aching pit
of titans falling into Tartaros as his knees nearly
    buckled,
but he steadied himself against his lover's shoulder.

Hadrian knowingly turned, smiled, and Antinous
    did not know
whether his flash of white teeth was the reassurance
    of love
or the smile of death from Hades at the side of
    Persephone.

The wailing was over, and heroes had passed into
    other realms,
while the spirits that had been called forth
    dissipated,
their forms coldly burned into his vision like brands
    of blue flame.

He was not sure who had spoken the chorus of
>   cries —
human priestesses or the Great Goddess Herself —
but he knew that hearing it, he had died and lived
>   again.

Demeter and Goetia:
The Eleusinian Mysteries and the Strange Case of Hadrian and Antinous

by P. Sufenas Virius Lupus

One of the terms used in classical Greek antiquity for a particular type of magic-user was *góes* (γοης), and their art or practice was known as goetia. As succinct a definition of goetia and the practice of the *góes* as may be possible is provided by Fritz Graf:

> A *góes* is a composite figure that combines ecstasy with ritual lament, healing, and divination. Plato connects his art with the activities of magi, seers, and initiators. Eros, he tells us in the *Symposium*, is the intermediary between the world of the gods and that of men, and that is why divination entirely belongs to him as well as "the art of the priests concerning sacrifices and initiations, just like incantations, prophecy in general, and magic goetia."[1]

While goetia is discussed in a variety of other primary and secondary sources from and about the ancient and late antique Mediterranean cultures, it attained a second life, as it were, with the later European grimoire traditions, and has been particularly associated with the summoning of demonic entities for magical purposes, often in the traditions associated with Solomonic ceremonial magic. Jake Stratton-Kent has endeavored (very successfully, I might add!) to take the tradition of goetia properly back to its classical sources in his two-volume work *Geosophia*,[2] and other modern works by practicing ceremonial magicians have also discussed goetia in interesting and effective manners.[3]

There is a stereotype amongst some academics, as well as some modern Hellenic polytheists, of the ancient Greek magician as a kind of anti-social and/or socially marginal figure that skulks around the peripheries of respectable society and religion, a counter-cultural or sub-cultural figure as much an outcast from those societies as modern magical practitioners are from modern society. Thus, it might seem strange to be speaking of goetia and the *góes* as figures that are in any manner connected to Demeter, the tutelary goddess of the Eleusinian Mysteries — a long-standing institution in Greek religion that is as much a part of the religious establishment of the ancient world as the major institutional branches of Christianity have been since the medieval period. However, there is a connection, and I suspect more might be drawn from that connection than may seem apparent at first glance.

Stratton-Kent comes close to discussing this connection at two points. On one occasion, he states:

> In the course of this study the origins of goetia are related to the practices of barbarian shamans, Thracian and Scythian. Among the former were ascetics whose morality and eschatology appear to have been potent influences on Pythagorean and Orphic teachings in Southern Italy and beyond. On the other hand the religious basis of both these schools can be traced to the cults of Demeter and Dionysus, incorporating Eastern influences.[4]

And, later,

> In classical antiquity the term goetia generally referred to rituals of an earlier phase of culture, or practices reflecting them. It deals particularly with the spirits of the underworld or of the earth, as opposed to heavenly or Ouranian deities and entities. These ranged from ghosts and demons to deities such as Demeter, Hades, and Persephone.[5]

While his fuller discussion touches on Demeter at various points, the most literal and basic connection between the *góes*, goetia, and Demeter is never mentioned in his otherwise excellent study.

This most literal and direct connection between Demeter and *góes* can be found in the *Home-*

ric Hymn to Demeter itself, on two occasions, associated with a mother's loss of a child. First, in line 82, Helios addresses Demeter, saying "But Goddess, give up for good your great lamentation."[6] The phrase for "great lamentation" is *mégan góon (μεγαν γοον)*,[7], which uses a form of the verb *góos*, from which *góes* and goetia are derived. The second instance involves Metaneira, the Eleusinian queen and mother of Demophoön, who cries out when she sees her son in the fire under Demeter's care, "Demophoön, my child, the stranger buries you / deep in the fire, causing me woe and bitter cares."[8] The word translated as "woe" is, again, *góon*.[9] Nancy Felson-Rubin and Harriet M. Deal comment on these parallel passages:

> The mourning of both Demeter for Persephone and Metaneira for Demophoön results in the ultimate release of each child from apparent death. It may well be that in these two contexts of the *Hymn* mourning has some magical efficacy. Compare the magical effect of Metaneira's intrusion itself on Demeter's ritual. Such magical efficacy might explain why Demeter goes into mourning several times in the course of her search for Persephone: by doing so, according to mythic logic, she might actually bring about Persephone's return from the dead. Such logic underlying her actions may be

valid even though the word *góos* only appears once for Demeter, and even though she may be quite unaware of the efficacy of her lamentation.[10]

Unfortunately, though they are right to point out the magical efficacy of Demeter and Metaneira's laments for their apparently lost children, Felson-Rubin and Deal do not seem to be aware of the actual magical practice and associations of the word *góos* with the *góes* and goetia. While it is likewise also possible that the author of the *Homeric Hymn to Demeter*, and likely as well the audience that would have heard or read it in antiquity, would have largely not taken the word in this case as necessarily implying goetia, nonetheless those versed in the traditions and practice of goetia probably would have heard these occasions of the word and connected it with their own "howlings," and their own ecstatic practices in relation to contact with chthonic deities and entities.

This brings us to the interesting case of Hadrian and Antinous in relation to Demeter, the Eleusinian Mysteries, and goetia. Hadrian was an initiate of the Eleusinian Mysteries on two occasions, achieving the senior grade of *epoptes*, and Antinous also seems to have been initiated once as a *mystes* before his death.[11] On the death of Antinous itself, the *Scriptores Historiae Augustae* (commonly

265

known as the *Historia Augusta*) has a curious line in relation to Hadrian:

Antinoum suum, dum per Nilum navigat, perdidit, quem muliebriter flevit.[12]

During a journey on the Nile he lost Antinous, his favourite, and for this youth he wept like a woman.[13]

While the translation above is a bit freer and more liberal in its details than the actual Latin text itself, nonetheless the important point for our consideration is the same in each case: at Antinous' death, Hadrian "wept like a woman." The author of the *Historia Augusta*, in this case, is making a comment on the inappropriateness of Hadrian's emotional reaction to his youthful lover's death, and particularly of his lamentation's negative view in the public eye. Since the author was writing for a Christian audience, it is meant to be that much more pejorative, and to even make comments on the lack of gender integrity it indicates about the great pagan Emperor. However, aside from those particular considerations, the detail is intriguing from the viewpoint of the present discussion, because it highlights something that might have been apparent to Hadrian and Antinous — and to Demeter and Persephone, as well as Metaneira and Demophoön, and any *góes* worth their salt — namely, that it may not only have been an emotional lament which was occurring on the part of the Emperor, but instead a magico-religious ritual intended to not only mourn for the loss of Antinous' life, but to ensure his continued existence in the afterlife, and Hadrian's further contact with him while the Emperor still lived and breathed upon the earth.

There have been suggestions in recent scholarly literature, particularly by Daniel Ogden, that perhaps Hadrian, under the influences of the Egyptian magician/priest/poet Pancrates or Pachrates of Heliopolis, engineered the sacrificial death of Antinous in order to have his own private daimon for necromantic purposes, working for him in the afterlife and divine realms.[14] While I do not personally think this is a likely scenario, given that Hadrian and Antinous were lovers, and Antinous had been a literal answer to Hadrian's prayers a number of years before,[15] nonetheless there might be some truth to the overall notion, with a vastly different motivation behind it and a very different framing of the historical events involved.

Not unlike Demeter, it is very possible that Hadrian lost Antinous completely unexpectedly and without any deliberate necromantic machinations on his part at all. Thus, his grief would have been genuine and expectable. It also seems likely, given that the apotheosis of victims who drown in the Nile was standard Egyptian practice at the time,[16] that Pancrates/Pachrates was on-hand and advised him on how such deification rituals would be done on behalf of the drowned youth. But, because Hadrian was a senior initiate of the Eleusinian Mysteries, and no doubt took part in some sort of ritual lament for Persephone's loss, and possibly that of Demophoön as well, and likewise Antinous would have done so with him when he had been initiated, perhaps the public mourning and lamentation that Hadrian did for Antinous — ostentatious and gender-inappropriate though it might have seemed to some viewers — was in fact an act of goetia which served to enliven Antinous' divine cultus in various locations throughout the Roman Empire, particularly in the Greek East where Antinous' cultus was vital and long-standing. It would have been thoroughly within the repertoire of the *góes*, counter-cultural though it may seem, to do something of that nature given the situation. Thus Hadrian, who was as much a fan of esoteric and magical practices as he was of conventional religion and of Greek culture generally speaking, might likewise have resorted to these methods as a way not only to commemorate his lover and to lament his loss, but to fix his presence and divine accessibility in the world at the crucial time after his death and deification in Egypt.

While the performance of most ecstatic religious practices, the arts of magic generally speaking, and of necromancy and divination in particular, are things which are seen as sinful within a Christian framework, perhaps the combination of these within the context of goetia ended up being considered especially contemptuous and dangerous within that theological milieu. Indeed, the "keening" over the dead in Ireland — a practice that occurred into the early twentieth century — was something uniquely Irish and which had roots deep within pre-Christian Irish culture, and was likewise looked upon with contempt and derision by the Christian churches in Ireland from the earliest periods.[17] In the Greek, Graeco-Roman, and Graeco-Egyptian contexts of late antiquity, perhaps the ritual lamentations over the dead likewise included elements that were derived from or fed into the complex of practices known as goetia. It further seems likely that these practices had as their divine etiology the laments of Demeter for Persephone, and on the level of human mythic precedent the laments of Metaneira for Demophoön as well, and that both of these precedents may have had their roles to play in the lore and continued ritual practices of the Eleusinian Mysteries. Thus, the association of all of these matters together, with the divine origins of the practice not coming from unknown Thracian or Scythian itinerant magicians, but instead the Goddess Demeter Herself, may have been powerful methodologies in the repertoire of those familiar with the Mysteries and with other magical practices, and would likewise have been threateningly dangerous connections to divine powers of an infernal and chthonic nature to certain mainstream cultural elements of late antiquity, and to the subsequent Christian religious hegemony as well.

Notes

1. Fritz Graf, *Magic in the Ancient World*, trans. Franklin Philip (Cambridge and London: Harvard University Press, 1999), p. 24.
2. Jake Stratton-Kent, *Geosophia: The Argo of Magic*, 2 volumes (Scarlet Imprint, 2010).
3. Alkistis Dimech and Peter Grey (eds.), *Howlings* (Scarlet Imprint, 2009).
4. Stratton-Kent, Volume 1, p. 42.
5. Stratton-Kent, Volume 2, p. 215.
6. Helene P. Foley (ed./trans.), *The Homeric Hymn to Demeter: Translation, Commentary, and Interpretive Essays* (Princeton: Princeton University Press, 1994), p. 6 line 82.
7. Foley, p. 7 line 82.
8. Foley, p. 14, lines 248-249.
9. Foley, p. 15, line 249.
10. Nancy Felson-Rubin and Harriet M. Deal, "Some Functions of the Demophoön Episode in the Homeric Hymn to Demeter," in Helene P. Foley (ed./trans.), *The Homeric Hymn to Demeter: Translation, Commentary, and Interpretive Essays* (Princeton: Princeton University Press, 1994), pp. 190-197 at 192n3.
11. P. Sufenas Virius Lupus, "'I Have Seen The Maiden': Hadrian, Antinous, and the Eleusinian

Mysteries," in Melitta Benu et al. (eds.), *Queen of the Sacred Way: A Devotional Anthology in Honor of Persephone* (Asheville, NC: Bibliotheca Alexandrina, 2012), pp. 164-172.

12. David Magie (ed./trans.), *The Scriptores Historiae Augustae*, 3 Volumes (Cambridge: Harvard University Press, 1921-1932), Hadrianus §14.5, Volume 1, p. 44.

13. Magie, Volume 1, p. 45.

14. Daniel Ogden, *Greek and Roman Necromancy* (Princeton: Princeton University Press, 2001), pp. 153-154; *Magic, Witchcraft, and Ghosts in the Greek and Roman Worlds: A Sourcebook* (Oxford and New York: Oxford University Press, 2002), pp. 250-251; *In Search of the Sorcerer's Apprentice: The Traditional Tales of Lucian's Lover of Lies* (Swansea: The Classical Press of Wales, 2007), pp. 249-251; *Night's Black Agents: Witches, Wizards and the Dead in the Ancient World* (New York and London: Hambledon Continuum, 2008), pp. 158-159. This is also echoed in Christian Day, *The Witches' Book of the Dead* (San Francisco: Red Wheel/Weiser, Inc., 2011), pp. 106-107, with Ogden's works as the likely source for the assertion.

15. P. Sufenas Virius Lupus, *Devotio Antinoo: The Doctor's Notes, Volume One* (The Red Lotus Library, 2011), pp. 348-349. Interestingly, Aphrodite Ourania and Eros are invoked in Hadrian's Thespaie Inscription, where he prays for a youthful lover; thus, this may further connect with the idea from

Plato's *Symposium* quoted earlier by Fritz Graf that Eros connects the divine and mortal worlds through divination, initiation, and goetia, amongst other things. Hadrian would have been familiar with Plato's writings without a doubt.

16. Jack Lindsay, *Men and Gods on the Roman Nile* (New York: Barnes & Noble, 1968), pp. 298-299 (and Lindsay's entire chapter on this subject, "The Blessed Drowned," pp. 297-314, is an extremely valuable resource on this topic); Theodor Abt and Erik Hornung, *Knowledge for the Afterlife: The Egyptian Amduat–A Quest for Immortality* (Zurich: Living Human Heritage Publications, 2003), pp. 116-119, 122; Robin Waterfield (trans.), *Herodotus: The Histories* (Oxford and New York: Oxford University Press, 1998), p. 128; Gil H. Renberg, "Hadrian and the Oracles of Antinous (SHA Hadr. 14.7); with an Appendix on the So-Called Antinoeion at Hadrian's Villa and Rome's Monte Pincio Obelisk," *Memoirs of the American Academy in Rome* 55 (2010), pp. 159-198.

17. See the sections in the "Old Irish Penitential" (a pre-9th century CE text), as given by Daniel Binchy's appendix to Ludwig Bieler (ed./trans.), *The Old Irish Pentitentials, Scriptores Latini Hiberniae* 5 (Dublin: Dublin Institute for Advanced Studies,), pp. 273-274 (§V.17, VI).

Mystery

by Janine Canan

You are the living Goddess
and I bow to You.
All the crickets chant ommmm
and the moon glows.

Time lies down
in the corpse pose.
And the Night births
hundreds of billions of galaxies.

You are the Mystery
without question or answer.
And we, the inevitable
explosion of Awe.

"The New Demeter":
The Syncretism of Diva Sabina Augusta to Demeter/Ceres

by P. Sufenas Virius Lupus

From the time of the accession of Octavian as the first Augustus and Emperor of Rome to the early third century CE, there were a total of seventeen women of the imperial families — usually, but not exclusively, the wives of the Emperors — who became syncretized to Demeter or Ceres in some fashion in coinage, statuary, or in surviving dedicatory inscriptions. While Octavian's wife Livia has the most such attestations surviving at present,[1] the runner-up is Diva Vibia Sabina Augusta, the wife of Hadrian.[2] Further, both her mother and grandmother, Diva Matidia and Diva Marciana respectively, also have surviving syncretistic depictions to Demeter/Ceres.[3] Some of these inscriptions call Sabina *néa Deméter*, the "New Demeter" (νεα Δημητηρ). The present brief survey will attempt to understand the various reasons why deified imperial women received this particular syncretism, and the attestations of it in relation to Diva Marciana and Diva Matidia (particularly the latter) as well as Diva Sabina, including further connections between them in other Hadrianic contexts.

In discussing inscriptions and other depictions which designate imperial women as the "New Demeter" or the "New Ceres," Barbette Stanley

Spaeth makes a distinction between associations created between the goddess and a given human individual, and assimilation of the human women to the goddess.

> In general direct assimilation to the goddess occurs only under two circumstances: when the woman represented is no longer living, or when the medium of representation is unofficial. After the death of a woman and her consecration as a diva, her assimilation to Ceres was not uncommon, even in official media such as state coinage....The assimilation of living women to Ceres in official media, however, is quite rare. It occurs only in state coinage for Agrippina the younger, the wife of Claudius, and for Sabina, the wife of Hadrian.[4]

After discussing a few more examples, and how representing a deceased woman assimilated to Ceres/Demeter would be acceptable since both are within the divine sphere in the Roman worldview, Spaeth returns to the matter of assimilation in unofficial media.

> In unofficial media, such as local coinage or private works of art, this distinction did not necessarily hold. Coins produced by local mints in various cities of the Empire fre-

quently show the living wife of the princeps with the attributes of Ceres….Similarly, local communities might honor such a woman with an inscription naming her as the "New Demeter"…[5]

Spaeth offers further examples of such dedications and depictions, and then concludes her discussion of such imperial women's assimilations to Demeter/Ceres as serving a variety of potential purposes, among them Demeter/Ceres being an ideal image of womanhood, and being associated with the ideal Roman feminine virtues of chastity (which encompasses much more than sexual purity for Romans, and included moral, ethical, and ritual purity as well as sexual purity and fidelity), motherhood, and female fertility. Further, these identifications could serve a variety of propagandistic purposes as well, including: the connection suggesting that the Emperor could provide grain for the entire Empire through his connection to the goddess as symbolized by his wife; an implication of the Emperor's support and upholding of and connection to the feminine virtues previously mentioned; Demeter/Ceres' role as a mother goddess bolstering imperial dynastic propaganda; and, finally, it may have legitimated the authority of the Emperor as *Pater Patriae* to have his wife depicted likewise as a *Mater Patriae* of the citizens of the Empire as-a-whole.[6]

However, some of these assertions are strange when it comes to Diva Sabina. Though Diva Marciana was the mother of Diva Matidia, and Diva Matidia was in turn the mother of Diva Sabina, Diva Sabina herself never had children, and may have been barren, which may have even been a cause for difficulties in the relationship of the Emperor and his Empress. While Hadrian himself was distantly related to his predecessor, Trajan, the line of Divae somewhat ensured Hadrian's legitimacy further — for there were questions about the validity of his accession to the principate after Trajan's death — by association with Trajan's sister Diva Marciana, and then his niece and great-niece Diva Matidia and Diva Sabina respectively. Continuing the portrayal of Demeter/Ceres imagery in the lineage of these imperial women, which began after the death of Trajan's sister during the final years of his principate, worked to prolong and bolster Hadrian's connection to Demeter/Ceres as the perfect image of feminine virtue.

Only one statue (now in Munich) and one official coin issue links Diva Marciana with Demeter/Ceres.[7] Her daughter, Diva Matidia, was syncretized to Demeter in one statue from Aphrodisias, now in Istanbul.[8] Diva Sabina Augusta, however, has a total of ten surviving syncretized or associated images or inscriptions of Demeter/Ceres: two inscriptions from Herakleia and Megara honoring her as the "New Demeter"; two inscriptions from

Athens and Tchelidjik honoring her as *Deméter Kaprophóros*, "Demeter the Bearer of Fruit"; one coin showing Sabina on the obverse and Ceres on the reverse issued during her lifetime; two coins (one during her life, one after her apotheosis) showing Sabina herself with Demeter/Ceres' attributes; and three statues (two from Ostia, one from Bulla Regia) showing Sabina as Ceres.[9] One of the statues of Diva Sabina in Ostia was found in a room opening onto the palaestra in Hadrian's Baths of Neptune which he founded in the city.[10]

In addition to these visual and inscriptional connections to Demeter/Ceres, Diva Sabina and her mother Diva Matidia had further connections in other contexts to Demeter and the Eleusinian Mysteries in particular. The Empress Sabina was probably initiated into the Eleusinian Mysteries in about 124 CE when her husband Hadrian was for the first time; immediately after this, her living syncretism to Demeter at Megara in the "New Demeter" inscription mentioned previously occurred.[11] Within a decade, while the Empress Sabina was still alive in late 130 CE, the death of Antinous caused Hadrian to found the city of Antinoöpolis at the spot in Egypt on the Nile where he drowned near Hermopolis. In the *phylai* and *demoi* names of the city, honor is given to (the then Diva) Matidia and the Empress Sabina. In the *phyla* named for Matidia, there are *demoi* named for her mother, Diva Marciana, and also Trajan's wife Diva Plotina, and two further *demoi* are called Demetrieus and Thesmophorios, which are named after Demeter and the Thesmophoria festival in that goddess' honor respectively. In the phyla named for Hadrian's wife, the Empress Sabina, there are *demoi* called Trophonieus, Phytalieus, and Gamelieus, which are all possibly connected to Eleusis and its traditions, and thus to Demeter as well.[12] Since Hadrian, Sabina, and Antinous were all initiates of the Eleusinian Mysteries,[13] the continued connection between them, and particularly between the women of the imperial family and the goddess Demeter, were important to commemorate in the new city and future cultus of the divine Antinous.

Appia Annia Regilla, a Roman woman who became the wife of the famed Athenian sophist, philanthropist, and Roman consul Herodes Attikos, was a priestess of Demeter Chamyne at Olympia, and as Demeter's priestess would have been the only woman allowed to watch the Olympic Games, with a front-row-seat to the spectacle. Regilla built a beautiful nymphaeum (fountain) at Olympia to provide the athletes and spectators with water, while likewise honoring the various current and recent Emperors and Empresses and her own family in a complex statuary program.[14] In a funerary cenotaph to Appia Annia Regilla near Rome, the poet Marcellus of Side commemorates her in a lengthy inscription which includes the following line: "The heavenly goddesses honor her, both the New Deo and the Old."[15] By the "New Deo" in that case and time, the Empress Diva Faustina the Elder, the deceased wife of the Emperor Antoninus Pius, was meant;[16] and the "Old Deo" was of course the goddess Demeter herself. Diva Sabina did not have the opportunity to be a priestess of Demeter during her lifetime, but in her syncretism to Demeter during her life and after her death, she had the opportunity to serve as the "New Deo" and living image of the goddess on behalf of the "Old Deo" to the entire citizenry of the Empire. Likewise, Diva Sabina Augusta had the opportunity to act in this role for the benefit of her husband, the Emperor Hadrian, after her death during the last years of his life and reign. While she may have lacked her own biological children, Diva Sabina as the New Demeter could have been the spiritual mother of every person in the Roman world through the Imperial Cultus which honored her in many locations across the Mediterranean world.

Notes

1. Barbette Stanley Spaeth, *The Roman Goddess Ceres* (Austin: University of Texas Press, 1996), pp. 169-173.
2. Spaeth, pp. 178-179.
3. Spaeth, pp. 177-178.
4. Spaeth, p. 120.
5. Spaeth, pp. 120-121.
6. Spaeth, pp. 121-122.

7. Spaeth, pp. 177-178.
8. Spaeth, p. 178.
9. Spaeth, pp. 178-179.
10. Mary Taliaferro Boatwright, *Hadrian and the Cities of the Roman Empire* (Princeton: Princeton University Press, 2003), p. 126n69.
11. Anthony R. Birley, *Hadrian: The Restless Emperor* (London and New York: Routledge, 2000), p. 178.
12. Boatwright, p. 194 note 124; Birley, pp. 254-255.
13. P. Sufenas Virius Lupus, 'I Have Seen The Maiden': Hadrian, Antinous, and the Eleusinian Mysteries," in Melitta Benu et al. (eds.), *Queen of the Sacred Way: A Devotional Anthology in Honor of Persephone* (Asheville, NC: Bibliotheca Alexandrina, 2012), pp. 164-172.
14. Sarah B. Pomeroy, *The Murder of Regilla: A Case of Domestic Violence in Antiquity* (Cambridge and London: Harvard University Press, 2007), pp. 87-103. While the information in this book is excellent and reliable, I cannot recommend nor endorse its overall viewpoint on the relationship of Regilla to her husband, or her potential murder.
15. Pomeroy, p. 170 line 6.
16. Spaeth, p. 179.

Prayer to Demeter

by Hester Butler-Ehle

Blessed Demeter,
you who are of the earth,
whose lineage lies as deep as stone within the soil,
who knows the sun upon the sod,
the seed beneath bare ground:
you are the hope of women and men,
you are the faith we keep in life and its sustaining.
Demeter,
great of mercy,
great of might,
you are the foundation of our existence,
the breath behind our being.
Yours it is to choose if we starve or are nourished,
if we survive or thrive.
Goddess most necessary,
goddess most dear,
we thank you for blessings rich and sundry,
we thank you for all we have,
for all we know.
Demeter, we call to you.

<u>Demeter</u>

by James Hall

In the fall of autumn leaves
the soft rustle
on fertile ground.
All our hopes are contained
within the seed.
Mother takes daughter by the hand
lightly treading,
with the knowledge that she —
that all —
must die.
There is no true sadness in death
for the sun and moon continue moving
and we will see each other
in the Fields of Elysium.

Appendix A: The Homeric Hymn II To Demeter
Translated by Hugh G. Evelyn-White

(ll. 1-3) I begin to sing of rich-haired Demeter, awful goddess — of her and her trim-ankled daughter whom Aidoneus rapt away, given to him by all-seeing Zeus the loud-thunderer.

(ll. 4-18) Apart from Demeter, lady of the golden sword and glorious fruits, she was playing with the deep-bosomed daughters of Oceanus and gathering flowers over a soft meadow, roses and crocuses and beautiful violets, irises also and hyacinths and the narcissus, which Earth made to grow at the will of Zeus and to please the Host of Many, to be a snare for the bloom-like girl — a marvellous, radiant flower. It was a thing of awe whether for deathless gods or mortal men to see: from its root grew a hundred blooms and is smelled most sweetly, so that all wide heaven above and the whole earth and the sea's salt swell laughed for joy. And the girl was amazed and reached out with both hands to take the lovely toy; but the wide-pathed earth yawned there in the plain of Nysa, and the lord, Host of Many, with his immortal horses sprang out upon her — the Son of Cronos, He who has many names (5).

(ll. 19-32) He caught her up reluctant on his golden car and bare her away lamenting. Then she cried out shrilly with her voice, calling upon her father, the Son of Cronos, who is most high and excellent. But no one, either of the deathless gods or of mortal men, heard her voice, nor yet the olive-trees bearing rich fruit: only tender-hearted Hecate, bright-coiffed, the daughter of Persaeus, heard the girl from her cave, and the lord Helios, Hyperion's bright son, as she cried to her father, the Son of Cronos. But he was sitting aloof, apart from the gods, in his temple where many pray, and receiving sweet offerings from mortal men. So he, that Son of Cronos, of many names, who is Ruler of Many and Host of Many, was bearing her away by leave of Zeus on his immortal chariot — his own brother's child and all unwilling.

(ll. 33-39) And so long as she, the goddess, yet beheld earth and starry heaven and the strong-flowing sea where fishes shoal, and the rays of the sun, and still hoped to see her dear mother and the tribes of the eternal gods, so long hope calmed her great heart for all her trouble.... ((LACUNA)) ....and the heights of the mountains and the depths of the sea rang with her immortal voice: and her queenly mother heard her.

(ll. 40-53) Bitter pain seized her heart, and she rent the covering upon her divine hair with her dear hands: her dark cloak she cast down from both her shoulders and sped, like a wild-bird, over the firm land and yielding sea, seeking her child. But no one would tell her the truth, neither god nor mortal men; and of the birds of omen none came with true news for her. Then for nine days queenly Deo wandered over the earth with flaming torches in her hands, so grieved that she never tasted ambrosia and the sweet draught of nectar, nor sprinkled her body with water. But when the tenth enlightening dawn had come, Hecate, with a torch in her hands, met her, and spoke to her and told her news:

(ll. 54-58) `Queenly Demeter, bringer of seasons and giver of good gifts, what god of heaven or what mortal man has rapt away Persephone and pierced with sorrow your dear heart? For I heard her voice, yet saw not with my eyes who it was. But I tell you truly and shortly all I know.'

(ll. 59-73) So, then, said Hecate. And the daughter of rich- haired Rhea answered her not, but sped swiftly with her, holding flaming torches in her hands. So they came to Helios, who is watchman of both gods and men, and stood in front of his horses: and the bright goddess enquired of him: `Helios, do you at least regard me, goddess as I am, if ever by word or deed of mine I have cheered your heart and spirit. Through the fruitless air I heard the thrilling cry of my daughter whom I bare, sweet scion of my body and lovely in form, as of one seized violently; though with my eyes I saw nothing. But you — for with your beams you look down from the bright upper air Over all the earth and sea — tell me truly of my dear child, if you have seen her anywhere, what god or mortal man has violently seized her against her will and mine, and so made off.'

(ll. 74-87) So said she. And the Son of Hyperion answered her: `Queen Demeter, daughter of rich-haired Rhea, I will tell you the truth; for I greatly reverence and pity you in your grief for your trim-ankled daughter. None other of the deathless gods is to blame, but only cloud-gathering Zeus who gave her to Hades, her father's brother, to be called his buxom wife. And Hades seized her and took her loudly crying in his chariot down to his realm of mist and gloom. Yet, goddess, cease your loud lament and keep not vain anger unrelentingly: Aidoneus, the Ruler of Many, is no unfitting husband among the deathless gods for your child, being your own brother and born of the same stock: also, for honour, he has that third share which he received when division was made at the first, and is appointed lord of those among whom he dwells.'

(ll. 88-89) So he spake, and called to his horses: and at his chiding they quickly whirled the swift chariot along, like long- winged birds.

(ll. 90-112) But grief yet more terrible and savage came into the heart of Demeter, and thereafter she was so angered with the dark-clouded Son of Cronos that she avoided the gathering of the gods and high Olympus, and went to the towns and rich fields of men, disfiguring her form a long while. And no one of men or deep-bosomed women knew her when they saw her, until she came to the house of wise Celeus who then was lord of fragrant Eleusis. Vexed in her dear heart, she sat near the wayside by the Maiden Well, from which the women of the place were used to draw water, in a shady place over which grew an olive shrub. And she was like an ancient woman who is cut off from childbearing and the gifts of garland-loving Aphrodite, like the nurses of king's children who deal justice, or like the house-keepers in their echoing halls. There the daughters of Celeus, son of Eleusis, saw her, as they were coming for easy-drawn water, to carry it in pitchers of bronze to their dear father's house: four were they and like goddesses in the flower of their girlhood, Callidice and Cleisidice and lovely Demo and Callithoe who was the eldest of them all. They knew her not, — for the gods are not easily discerned by mortals — but standing near by her spoke winged words:

(ll. 113-117) `Old mother, whence and who are you of folk born long ago? Why are you gone away from the city and do not draw near the houses? For there in the shady halls are women of just such age as you, and others younger; and they would welcome you both by word and by deed.'

(ll. 118-144) Thus they said. And she, that queen among goddesses answered them saying: `Hail, dear children, whosoever you are of woman-kind. I will tell you my story; for it is not unseemly that I should tell you truly what you ask. Doso is my name, for my stately mother gave it me. And now I am come from Crete over the sea's wide back, -- not willingly; but pirates brought be thence by force of strength against my liking. Afterwards they put in with their swift craft to Thoricus, and there the women landed on the shore in full throng and the men likewise, and they began to make ready a meal by the stern-cables of the ship. But my heart craved not pleasant food, and I fled secretly across the dark country and escaped by masters, that they should not take me unpurchased across the sea, there to win a price for me. And so I wandered and am come here: and I know not at all what land this is or what people are in it. But may all those who dwell on Olympus give you husbands and birth of children as parents desire, so you take pity on me, maidens, and show me this clearly that I may learn, dear children, to the house of what man and woman I may go, to work for them cheerfully at such tasks as belong to a woman of my age. Well could I nurse a new born child, holding him in my arms, or keep house, or spread my masters' bed in a recess of the well-built chamber, or teach the women their work.'

(ll. 145-146) So said the goddess. And straightway the unwed maiden Callidice, goodliest in form of the daughters of Celeus, answered her and said:

(ll. 147-168) 'Mother, what the gods send us, we mortals bear perforce, although we suffer; for they are much stronger than we. But now I will teach you clearly, telling you the names of men who have great power and honour here and are chief among the people, guarding our city's coif of towers by their wisdom and true judgements: there is wise Triptolemus and Dioclus and Polyxeinus and blameless Eumolpus and Dolichus and our own brave father. All these have wives who manage in the house, and no one of them, so soon as she has seen you, would dishonour you and turn you from the house, but they will welcome you; for indeed you are godlike. But if you will, stay here; and we will go to our father's house and tell Metaneira, our deep-bosomed mother, all this matter fully, that she may bid you rather come to our home than search after the houses of others. She has an only son, late-born, who is being nursed in our well-built house, a child of many prayers and welcome: if you could bring him up until he reached the full measure of youth, any one of womankind who should see you would straightway envy you, such gifts would our mother give for his upbringing.'

(ll. 169-183) So she spake: and the goddess bowed her head in assent. And they filled their shining vessels with water and carried them off rejoicing. Quickly they came to their father's great house and straightway told their mother according as they had heard and seen. Then she bade them go with all speed and invite the stranger to come for a measureless hire. As hinds or heifers in spring time, when sated with pasture, bound about a meadow, so they, holding up the folds of their lovely garments, darted down the hollow path, and their hair like a crocus flower streamed about their shoulders. And they found the good goddess near the wayside where they had left her before, and led her to the house of their dear father. And she walked behind, distressed in her dear heart, with her head veiled and wearing a dark cloak which waved about the slender feet of the goddess.

(ll. 184-211) Soon they came to the house of heaven-nurtured Celeus and went through the portico to where their queenly mother sat by a pillar of the close-fitted roof, holding her son, a tender scion, in her bosom. And the girls ran to her. But the goddess walked to the threshold: and her head reached the roof and she filled the doorway with a heavenly radiance. Then awe and reverence and pale fear took hold of Metaneira, and she rose up from her couch before Demeter, and bade her be seated. But Demeter, bringer of seasons and giver of perfect gifts, would not sit upon the bright couch, but stayed silent with lovely eyes cast down until careful Iambe placed a jointed seat for her and threw over it a silvery fleece. Then she sat down and held her veil in her hands before her face. A long time she sat upon the stool (6) without speaking because of her sorrow, and greeted no one by word or by sign, but rested, never smiling, and tasting neither food nor drink, because she pined with longing for her deep-bosomed daughter, until careful Iambe — who pleased her moods in aftertime also — moved the holy lady with many a quip and jest to smile and laugh and cheer her heart. Then Metaneira filled a cup with sweet wine and offered it to her; but she refused it, for she said it was not lawful for her to drink red wine, but bade them mix meal and water with soft mint and give her to drink. And Metaneira mixed the draught and gave it to the goddess as she bade. So the great queen Deo received it to observe the sacrament.... (7) ((LACUNA))

(ll. 212-223) And of them all, well-girded Metaneira first began to speak: `Hail, lady! For I think you are not meanly but nobly born; truly dignity and grace are conspicuous upon your eyes as in the eyes of kings that deal justice. Yet we mortals bear perforce what the gods send us, though we be grieved; for a yoke is set upon our necks. But now, since you are come here, you shall have what I can bestow: and nurse me this child whom the gods gave me in my old age and beyond my hope, a son much prayed for. If you should bring him up until he reach the full measure of youth, any one of womankind that sees you will straightway envy you, so great reward would I give for his upbringing.'

(ll. 224-230) Then rich-haired Demeter answered her: 'And to you, also, lady, all hail, and may the gods give you good! Gladly will I take the boy to my breast, as you bid me, and will nurse him. Never, I ween, through any heedlessness of his nurse shall witchcraft hurt him nor yet the Undercutter (8): for I know a charm far stronger than the Woodcutter, and I know an excellent safeguard against woeful witchcraft.'

(ll. 231-247) When she had so spoken, she took the child in her fragrant bosom with her divine hands: and his mother was glad in her heart. So the goddess nursed in the palace Demophoon, wise Celeus' goodly son whom well-girded Metaneira bare. And the child grew like some immortal being, not fed with food nor nourished at the breast: for by day rich-crowned Demeter would anoint him with ambrosia as if he were the offspring of a god and breathe sweetly upon him as she held him in her bosom. But at night she would hide him like a brand in the heard of the fire, unknown to his dear parents. And it wrought great wonder in these that he grew beyond his age; for he was like the gods face to face. And she would have made him deathless and unageing, had not well-girded Metaneira in her heedlessness kept watch by night from her sweet-smelling chamber and spied. But she wailed and smote her two hips, because she feared for her son and was greatly distraught in her heart; so she lamented and uttered winged words:

(ll. 248-249) 'Demophoön, my son, the strange woman buries you deep in fire and works grief and bitter sorrow for me.'

(ll. 250-255) Thus she spoke, mourning. And the bright goddess, lovely-crowned Demeter, heard her, and was wroth with her. So with her divine hands she snatched from the fire the dear son whom Metaneira had born unhoped-for in the palace, and cast him from her to the ground; for she was terribly angry in her heart. Forthwith she said to well-girded Metaneira:

(ll. 256-274) 'Witless are you mortals and dull to foresee your lot, whether of good or evil, that comes upon you. For now in your heedlessness you have wrought folly past healing; for — be witness the oath of the gods, the relentless water of Styx — I would have made your dear son deathless and unaging all his days and would have bestowed on him everlasting honour, but now he can in no way escape death and the fates. Yet shall unfailing honour always rest upon him, because he lay upon my knees and slept in my arms. But, as the years move round and when he is in his prime, the sons of the Eleusinians shall ever wage war and dread strife with one another continually. Lo! I am that Demeter who has share of honour and is the greatest help and cause of joy to the undying gods and mortal men. But now, let all the people build be a great temple and an altar below it and beneath the city and its sheer wall upon a rising hillock above Callichorus. And I myself will teach my rites, that hereafter you may reverently perform them and so win the favour of my heart.'

(ll. 275-281) When she had so said, the goddess changed her stature and her looks, thrusting old age away from her: beauty spread round about her and a lovely fragrance was wafted from her sweet-smelling robes, and from the divine body of the goddess a light shone afar, while golden tresses spread down over her shoulders, so that the strong house was filled with brightness as with lightning. And so she went out from the palace.

(ll. 281-291) And straightway Metaneira's knees were loosed and she remained speechless for a long while and did not remember to take up her late-born son from the ground. But his sisters heard his pitiful wailing and sprang down from their well-spread beds: one of them took up the child in her arms and laid him in her bosom, while another revived the fire, and a third rushed with soft feet to bring their mother from her fragrant chamber. And they gathered about the struggling child and washed him, embracing him lovingly; but he was not comforted, because nurses and handmaids much less skilful were holding him now.

(ll. 292-300) All night long they sought to appease the glorious goddess, quaking with fear. But, as soon as dawn began to show, they told powerful Celeus all things without fail, as the lovely-crowned goddess Demeter charged them. So Celeus called the countless people to an assembly and bade them make a goodly temple for rich-haired Demeter and an altar upon the rising hillock. And they obeyed him right speedily and harkened to his voice, doing as he commanded. As for the child, he grew like an immortal being.

(ll. 301-320) Now when they had finished building and had drawn back from their toil, they went every man to his house. But golden-haired Demeter sat there apart from all the blessed gods and stayed, wasting with yearning for her deep-bosomed daughter. Then she caused a most dreadful and cruel year for mankind over the all-nourishing earth: the ground would not make the seed sprout, for rich-crowned Demeter kept it hid. In the fields the oxen drew many a curved plough in vain, and much white barley was cast upon the land without avail. So she would have destroyed the whole race of man with cruel famine and have robbed them who dwell on Olympus of their glorious right of gifts and sacrifices, had not Zeus perceived and marked this in his heart. First he sent golden-winged Iris to call rich-haired Demeter, lovely in form. So he commanded. And she obeyed the dark-clouded Son of Cronos, and sped with swift feet across the space between. She came to the stronghold of fragrant Eleusis, and there finding dark-cloaked Demeter in her temple, spake to her and uttered winged words:

(ll. 321-323) 'Demeter, father Zeus, whose wisdom is everlasting, calls you to come join the tribes of the eternal gods: come therefore, and let not the message I bring from Zeus pass unobeyed.'

(ll. 324-333) Thus said Iris imploring her. But Demeter's heart was not moved. Then again the father sent forth all the blessed and eternal gods besides: and they came, one after the other, and kept calling her and offering many very beautiful gifts and whatever right she might be pleased to choose among the deathless gods. Yet no one was able to persuade her mind and will, so wrath was she in her heart; but she stubbornly rejected all their words:

for she vowed that she would never set foot on fragrant Olympus nor let fruit spring out of the ground, until she beheld with her eyes her own fair-faced daughter.

(ll. 334-346) Now when all-seeing Zeus the loud-thunderer heard this, he sent the Slayer of Argus whose wand is of gold to Erebus, so that having won over Hades with soft words, he might lead forth chaste Persephone to the light from the misty gloom to join the gods, and that her mother might see her with her eyes and cease from her anger. And Hermes obeyed, and leaving the house of Olympus, straightway sprang down with speed to the hidden places of the earth. And he found the lord Hades in his house seated upon a couch, and his shy mate with him, much reluctant, because she yearned for her mother. But she was afar off, brooding on her fell design because of the deeds of the blessed gods. And the strong Slayer of Argus drew near and said:

(ll. 347-356) `Dark-haired Hades, ruler over the departed, father Zeus bids me bring noble Persephone forth from Erebus unto the gods, that her mother may see her with her eyes and cease from her dread anger with the immortals; for now she plans an awful deed, to destroy the weakly tribes of earthborn men by keeping seed hidden beneath the earth, and so she makes an end of the honours of the undying gods. For she keeps fearful anger and does not consort with the gods, but sits aloof in her fragrant temple, dwelling in the rocky hold of Eleusis.'

(ll. 357-359) So he said. And Aidoneus, ruler over the dead, smiled grimly and obeyed the behest of Zeus the king. For he straightway urged wise Persephone, saying:

(ll. 360-369) 'Go now, Persephone, to your dark-robed mother, go, and feel kindly in your heart towards me: be not so exceedingly cast down; for I shall be no unfitting husband for you among the deathless gods, that am own brother to father Zeus. And while you are here, you shall rule all that lives and moves and shall have the greatest rights among the deathless gods: those who defraud you and do not appease your power with offerings, reverently performing rites and paying fit gifts, shall be punished for evermore.'

(ll. 370-383) When he said this, wise Persephone was filled with joy and hastily sprang up for gladness. But he on his part secretly gave her sweet pomegranate seed to eat, taking care for himself that she might not remain continually with grave, dark-robed Demeter. Then Aidoneus the Ruler of Many openly got ready his deathless horses beneath the golden chariot. And she mounted on the chariot, and the strong Slayer of Argos took reins and whip in his dear hands and drove forth from the hall, the horses speeding readily. Swiftly they traversed their long course, and neither the sea nor river-waters nor grassy glens nor mountain- peaks checked the career of the immortal horses, but they clave the deep air above them as they went. And Hermes brought them to the place where rich-crowned Demeter was staying and checked them before her fragrant temple.

(ll. 384-404) And when Demeter saw them, she rushed forth as does a Maenad down some thick-wooded mountain, while Persephone on the other side, when she saw her mother's sweet eyes, left the chariot and horses, and leaped down to run to her, and falling upon her neck, embraced her. But while Demeter was still holding her dear child in her arms, her heart suddenly misgave her for some snare, so that she feared greatly and ceased fondling her daughter and asked of her at once: `My child, tell me, surely you have not tasted any food while you were below? Speak out and hide nothing, but let us both know. For if you have not, you shall come back from loathly Hades and live with me and your father, the dark-clouded Son of Cronos and be honoured by all the deathless gods; but if you have tasted food, you must go back again beneath the secret places of the earth, there to dwell a third part of the seasons every year: yet for the two parts you shall be with me and the other deathless gods. But when the earth shall bloom with the fragrant flowers of spring in every kind, then from the realm of darkness and gloom thou shalt come up once more to be a wonder for gods and mortal men. And now tell me how he rapt you away to the realm of darkness and gloom, and by what trick did the strong Host of Many beguile you?'

(ll. 405-433) Then beautiful Persephone answered her thus: 'Mother, I will tell you all without error. When luck-bringing Hermes came, swift messenger from my father the Son of Cronos and the other Sons of Heaven, bidding me come back from Erebus that you might see me with your eyes and so cease from your anger and fearful wrath against the gods, I sprang up at once for joy; but he secretly put in my mouth sweet food, a pomegranate seed, and forced me to taste against my will. Also I will tell how he rapt me away by the deep plan of my father the Son of Cronos and carried me off beneath the depths of the earth, and will relate the whole matter as you ask. All we were playing in a lovely meadow, Leucippe (9) and Phaeno and Electra and Ianthe, Melita also and Iache with Rhodea and Callirhoe and Melobosis and Tyche and Ocyrhoe, fair as a flower, Chryseis, Ianeira, Acaste and Admete and Rhodope and Pluto and charming Calypso; Styx too was there and Urania and lovely Galaxaura with Pallas who rouses battles and Artemis delighting in arrows: we were playing and gathering sweet flowers in our hands, soft crocuses mingled with irises and hyacinths, and rose-blooms and lilies, marvellous to see, and the narcissus which the wide earth caused to grow yellow as a crocus. That I plucked in my joy; but the earth parted beneath, and there the strong lord, the Host of Many, sprang forth and in his golden chariot he bore me away, all unwilling, beneath the earth: then I cried with a shrill cry. All this is true, sore though it grieves me to tell the tale.'

(ll. 434-437) So did they turn, with hearts at one, greatly cheer each the other's soul and spirit with many an embrace: their heart had relief from their griefs while each took and gave back joyousness.

(ll. 438-440) Then bright-coiffed Hecate came near to them, and often did she embrace the daughter of holy Demeter: and from that time the lady Hecate was minister and companion to Persephone.

(ll. 441-459) And all-seeing Zeus sent a messenger to them, rich-haired Rhea, to bring dark-cloaked Demeter to join the families of the gods: and he promised to give her what right she should choose among the deathless gods and agreed that her daughter should go down for the third part of the circling year to darkness and gloom, but for the two parts should live with her mother and the other deathless gods. Thus he commanded. And the goddess did not disobey the message of Zeus; swiftly she rushed down from the peaks of Olympus and came to the plain of Rharus, rich, fertile corn-land once, but then in nowise fruitful, for it lay idle and utterly leafless, because the white grains was hidden by design of trim-ankled Demeter. But afterwards, as springtime waxed, it was soon to be waving with long ears of corn, and its rich furrows to be loaded with grain upon the ground, while others would already be bound in sheaves. There first she landed from the fruitless upper air: and glad were the goddesses to see each other and cheered in heart. Then bright- coiffed Rhea said to Demeter:

(ll. 460-469) `Come, my daughter; for far-seeing Zeus the loud-thunderer calls you to join the families of the gods, and has promised to give you what rights you please among the deathless gods, and has agreed that for a third part of the circling year your daughter shall go down to darkness and gloom, but for the two parts shall be with you and the other deathless gods: so has he declared it shall be and has bowed his head in token. But come, my child, obey, and be not too angry unrelentingly with the dark-clouded Son of Cronos; but rather increase forthwith for men the fruit that gives them life.'

(ll. 470-482) So spake Rhea. And rich-crowned Demeter did not refuse but straightway made fruit to spring up from the rich lands, so that the whole wide earth was laden with leaves and flowers. Then she went, and to the kings who deal justice, Triptolemus and Diocles, the horse-driver, and to doughty Eumolpus and Celeus, leader of the people, she showed the conduct of her rites and taught them all her mysteries, to Triptolemus and Polyxeinus and Diocles also, — awful mysteries which no one may in any way transgress or pry into or utter, for deep awe of the gods checks the voice. Happy is he among men upon earth who has seen these mysteries; but he who is uninitiate and who has no part in them, never has lot of like good things once he is dead, down in the darkness and gloom.

(ll. 483-489) But when the bright goddess had taught them all, they went to Olympus to the gathering of the other gods. And there they dwell beside Zeus who delights in thunder, awful and reverend goddesses. Right blessed is he among men on earth whom they freely love: soon they do send Plutus as guest to his great house, Plutus who gives wealth to mortal men.

(ll. 490-495) And now, queen of the land of sweet Eleusis and sea-girt Paros and rocky Antron, lady, giver of good gifts, bringer of seasons, queen Deo, be gracious, you and your daughter all beauteous Persephone, and for my song grant me heart-cheering substance. And now I will remember you and another song also.

Appendix B: The Orphic Hymns to Demeter

Orphic Hymn 40 to Demeter (translated by Thomas Taylor) (Greek hymns C3rd B.C. to 2nd A.D.) :

To Demeter Eleusinia. O universal mother, Deo famed, august, the source of wealth, and various named: great nurse, all-bounteous, blessed and divine, who joyest in peace; to nourish corn is thine. Goddess of seed, of fruits abundant, fair, harvest and threshing are thy constant care. Lovely delightful queen, by all desired, who dwellest in Eleusis' holy vales retired. Nurse of all mortals, who benignant mind first ploughing oxen to the yoke confined; and gave to men what nature's wants require, with plenteous means of bliss, which all desire. In verdure flourishing, in glory bright, assessor of great Bromios [Dionysos] bearing light: rejoicing in the reapers' sickles, kind, whose nature lucid, earthly, pure, we find. Prolific, venerable, nurse divine, thy daughter loving, holy Koure [Persephone]. A car with Drakones (Dragon-Serpents) yoked 'tis thine to guide, and, orgies singing, round thy throne to ride. Only-begotten, much-producing queen, all flowers are thine, and fruits of lovely green. Bright Goddess, come, with summer's rich increase swelling and pregnant, leading smiling peace; come with fair concord and imperial health, and join with these a needful store of wealth.

Orphic Hymn 41 to Demeter (translated by Thomas Taylor) (Greek hymns C3rd B.C. to 2nd A.D.):

To Meter Antaia (Cerulean Mother) [Demeter]. Basileia Antaia (Cerulean Queen) [Demeter], of celebrated name, from whom both men and Gods immortal came; who widely wandering once, oppressed with grief, in Eleusis' valleys foundest relief, discovering Persephone thy daughter pure in dread Aides (Haides), dismal and obscure. A sacred youth while through the earth you stray, Dysaulos [Iakkhos], attending leader of the way; the holy marriage Khthonios Zeus [Haides] relating, while oppressed with grief you rove. Come, much invoked, and to these rites inclined, thy mystic suppliant bless, with favouring mind.

Appendix C: Hymn VI to Demeter

Callimachus, *Hymn 6 to Demeter* (translated by A.W. Mair) (Greek poet C3rd B.C.): [Ostensibly a hymn for the Thesmophoria festival of Athens:] As the Basket comes, greet it, ye women, saying 'Demeter, greatly hail! Lady of much bounty, of many measures of corn.' As the Basket comes, from the ground shall ye behold it, ye uninitiated, and gaze not from the roof or from aloft — child nor wife nor maid hath shed her hair [i.e. the locks were dedicated at puberty] — neither then nor when we spit from parched mouths fasting [i.e. the Nesteia, the second day of the Thesmophoria, a day of fasting]. Hesperos [the star Venus] from the clouds marks the time of its coming: Hesperos (the Evening Star), who alone persuaded Demeter to drink, what time she pursued the unknown tracks of her stolen daughter [Persephone].

Lady, how were thy feet able to carry thee unto the West, unto the Melanoi (Black Men) and where the golden apples are? Thou didst not drink nor dist thou eat during that time nor didst thou wash. Thrice didst thou cross Akheloios with his silver eddies, and as often didst thou pass over each of the ever-flowing rivers, and thrice didst thou seat thee on the ground beside the fountain Kallikhoros (Callichorus) [i.e. the well at Eleusis], parched and without drinking, and didst not eat nor wash.

Nay, nay, let us not speak of that which brought the tear to Deo! Better to tell how she gave cities pleasing ordinances; better to tell how she was the first to cut straw and holy sheaves of corn-ears and put in oxen to tread them, what time Triptolemos was taught the good craft . . .

O Demeter, never may that man be my friend who is hateful to thee, nor ever may he share party-wall with me; ill neighbours I abhor.

Sing, ye maidens, and ye mothers, say with them : 'Damater, greatly hail! Lady of much bounty, of many measures of corn.' And as the four white-haired horses convey the Basket, so unto us will the great goddess of wide dominion come brining white spring and white harvest and winter and autumn, and keep us to another year. And as unsandalled and with hair unbound we walk the city, so shall we have foot and head unharmed for ever. And as the van-bearers bear vans [i.e. skull-shaped baskets, sued for offering first-fruits to the gods] full of gold, so may we get gold unstinted. Far as the City Chambers let the uninitiated follow, but the initiated even unto the very shrine of the goddess — as many as are under sixty years. But show that are heavy and she that stretches her hand to Eileithyia [goddess of childbirth] and she that is in pain — sufficient it is that they go so far as their knees are able.

And to them Deo shall give all things to overflowing, even as if they came unto her temple.

Hail, goddess, and save this people in harmony and in prosperity, and in the fields bring us all pleasant things! Feed our kine, bring us flocks, bring us the corn-ear, bring us harvest! And nurse peace, that he who sows may also reap. Be gracious, O thrice-prayed for, great Queen of goddesses!

Appendix D: Our Contributors

Mike Alexander's full-length collection, *Retrograde*, is available at pandjpoetics.com. His chapbook, *We Internet in Different Voices* (*Modern Metrics*) can be ordered through *EXOT* books (http://www.exot.typepad.com/exotbooks/). His poems have also appeared recently in *River Styx, Measure, Raintown Review, Abridged, The Nervous Breakdown*, & other journals.

Katie Anderson is a writer and poet living in the United States. She is also acting editor for *ShadowNexus Publications*. Her poetry has been published in the U.S. and abroad. She is deeply passionate about the study of mythology and ancient religion, as it is a major influence in her poetry. She is also interested in the development of personalized mythologies in the modern world.

Michelle Auerbach is the author of *The Third Kind of Horse* (2013 *Beatdom Books*). Her writing has appeared in (among other places) *The New York Times, The Guardian, The Denver Quarterly, Chelsea Magazine, Bombay Gin*, and the literary anthologies *The Veil* (*UC Berkley Press*), *Uncontained Baksun Books*, and *You.: An Anthology of Essays in the Second Person* (*Welcome Table Press*). She is the winner of the 2011 Northern Colorado Fiction Prize. www.michelleauerbach.com.

Brandi Auset is a High Priestess of the Goddess, a Reiki Master Teacher and spiritual counselor. She is the author of *The Goddess Guide: Exploring the Attributes and Correspondences of the Divine Feminine* (*Llewellyn*, 2009) and teaches workshops on many topics, including techniques for infusing the Goddess and Her power into daily life and spiritual practice.

Christa A. Bergerson has been worshipping and adoring the wondrous Roman-Greco-Egyptian Gods since she was a precocious tot. She is also an occultist, an environmentalist, and a Guardian of those who writhe betwixt the veil. In her spare time, she enjoys listening to phonographs, traversing the sparse wilds of Illinois, and swimming in the dead of night. Her intuited poetry has appeared in *Waters of Life*, *Bearing Torches*, *The Beltane Papers*, *Abyss & Apex*, *Circle Magazine*, and *Faerie Nation Magazine*, among other publications. For astral and/or sublunary communication feel free to contact her at carmentaeternus@comcast.net

Erzabet Bishop has been crafting stories since she could pound keys on her parent's old typewriter. She has only just learned that it is a whole lot more fun writing naughty books. She is a contributing author to the *Silk Words* website, *A Christmas To Remember*, *Sweat*, *When the Clock Strikes Thirteen*,

Unbound Box, *Milk & Cookies & Handcuffs*, *Holidays in Hell*, *Corset Magazine: Sex Around the World Issue* and *Man vs. Machine: The Sex Toy Issue*, *Smut by the Sea Volume 2*, *Hell Whore Volume 2*, *Can't Get Enough* (upcoming, Cleis), *Slave Girls* (upcoming, Cleis) *Anything She Wants*, *Dirty Little Numbers*, *Kink-E magazine*, *Coming Together: Girl on Girl*, *Shifters* and *Coming Together: Hungry for Love* among others. She is the author of *Lipstick*, *Dinner Date*, *Sigil Fire*, The *Erotic Pagans Series: Beltane Fires*, *Samhain Shadows* and *Yuletide Temptation*. She lives in Texas with her husband, furry children and can often be found lurking in local bookstores. She loves to bake, make naughty crochet projects and watch monster movies.

Melia Brokaw is a Librarian, Housewife, Mother, Wife, Devotee to Zeus and Isis, Writer, Crafter and Woman. She is an octopus with many tentacles of interest making her way through the sea of life. Editor of *From Cave to Sky*, another book in the *Biblotheca Alexandrina* line up, under the name Melia Suez.
Personal Blog: 4ofwands.wordpress.com.
Author Blog: OakenScrolls.wordpress.com.

Rebecca Buchanan is the editor of *Eternal Haunted Summer*, a Pagan literary ezine, and editor-in-chief of *Biblotheca Alexandrina*. She has been published in a variety of venues, including *Cliterature*,

Datura, The Future Fire, Linguistic Erosion, Luna Station Quarterly, and *Mandragora*. She blogs regularly at BookMusing: (Re)Discovering Pagan Literature.

Hester Butler-Ehle is a polytheist who has loved the Greek gods ever since she was a young girl reading Edith Hamilton. She has been a devotee of Aphrodite for over fifteen years; she prefers Hesiod to Homer and Sappho to all other poetry.

Janine Canan is the author of twenty books including *Ardor: Poems of Life* and, forthcoming, *Love Is My Religion: Essential Teachings of Mata Amritanandamayi*; award-winning anthologies, *She Rises like the Sun* and *Messages from Amma*; music-inspiring translations of French poet Francis Jammes and German Jewish poet Else Lasker-Schüler; as well as essays, *Goddesses Goddesses*, and illustrated stories, *Journeys with Justine* and *Walk Now in Beauty*, read in the Navajo Literacy Project. Her work appears widely in journals, anthologies, films, public programs, on radio, television and internet. Born in La Ciudad de la Reina de los Angeles, Dr. Canan graduated from Stanford University with distinction and New York University School of Medicine. She is a private psychiatrist in Sonoma, California. Visit JanineCanan.com for more information.

Fern G.Z. Carr is a lawyer, teacher, and past president of the local branch of the BC Society for the Prevention of Cruelty to Animals. She is a member of the League of Canadian Poets and former Poet-in-Residence who composes and translates poetry in five languages. A winner of national and international poetry contests, Carr has been nominated for the 2013 Pushcart Prize. She has been published extensively worldwide, from Finland to the Seychelles, including India where she has been cited as a contributor to the Prakalpana literary movement. Some of Carr's poetry has been assigned reading for the West Virginia University's College of Law course entitled "Lawyers, Poets, and Poetry." Canadian honours include being featured online in Canada's national newspaper, *The Globe and Mail*, having her poetry set to music by a Juno-nominated musician, and having her poem "I Am" chosen by the Parliamentary Poet Laureate as Poem of the Month for Canada. One of Carr's haiku is even included on a DVD sent to Mars on NASA's MAVEN spacecraft. www.ferngzcarr.com

Dawn Corrigan's poetry and prose have appeared in a number of print and online journals and anthologies. Her debut novel, an environmental mystery called *Mitigating Circumstances*, was released by Five Star/Cengage in December 2013. She lives in Gulf Breeze, Florida.

C.D. Coss is a writer working in northern Indiana.

James E. Hall has been previously published in *The Blue Hour* and *poeticdiversity*. He lives in Northern Virginia with his family, and works in a number of roles within the technology industry. His concept of Demeter is inspired by his wife and her own faith in the Mysteries.

Marie Kane's poetry has been twice nominated for a Pushcart Prize and has appeared in the *Bellevue Literary Review, U. S. 1 Worksheets, Wordgathering, The Schuylkill Valley Journal, Naugatuck River Review, The Meadowland Review, I-70 Review, Small Print Magazine, Adanna Literary Journal*, the *Damselfly Press,* and many others. Her work has been frequently anthologized and has placed in the top three in several competitions: the Poetry Society of New Hampshire contest, the Inglis House contest, the D&R Greenway contest, and the Robert Frasier. She is the final juror in the national scholastic Sarah Mook poetry contest, grades K-12. Her chapbook, *Survivors in the Garden* (Big Table Publishing, 2012), centers on her life with multiple sclerosis. She is the 2006 Bucks County (PA) Poet Laureate and the poetry editor for *Pentimento Magazine*. See more of her work at www.mariekanepoetry.com.

Kim King was born and raised in Lockport, New York. She lived and studied in France and now teaches French in a Central Pennsylvania high school. She is currently enrolled in the MA in Writing Program at The Johns Hopkins University. Her poems have appeared in the book *Prompted: An International Collection of Poems*, *River Poets Journal*, *Stone Mountain Review*, *Outside in Literary and Travel Magazine*, *Wild Onions 2014*, and *Poetic Asides*. Kim's poems have been included in the recently published anthologies *Point Mass*, *In Gilded Frame*, and *Poetic Bloomings: the first year*.

Jennifer Lawrence likes doing things the hard way, which explains most of how her life has turned out. After earning a B.A. in Literature and a B.S. in Criminal Justice, she has gone on to work as an editor for *Jupiter Gardens Press*, a small publishing company in the Midwest. Her interests include history, gardening, herbalism, mythology and fairy tales, hiking, camping, and the martial arts. Her work has appeared in numerous publications, including *Aphelion*, *Jabberwocky*, *Cabinet Des Fees*, *Goblin Fruit*, *Idunna*, *Oak Leaves*, and many devotional anthologies. A multi-trad pagan, she has venerated the gods of Greece, Ireland, and the Northlands for decades now; aside from membership in Hellenion, she is also a member of The Troth, Ár nDraíocht Féin, and Ord Brigideach. She lives with five cats, an overgrown garden full of nature spirits, and a houseful of gargoyles somewhere outside of Chicago.

Gerri Leen lives in Northern Virginia and originally hails from Seattle. She has a collection of short stories, *Life Without Crows*, out from *Hadley Rille Books*, and stories and poems published in such places as: *Sword and Sorceress XXIII*, *Spinetinglers*, *Entrances and Exits*, *She Nailed a Stake Through His Head*, *Dia de los Muertos*, *Return to Luna*, *Triangulation: Dark Glass*, *Sails & Sorcery*, and *Paper Crow*. Visit http://www.gerrileen.com to see what else she's been up to.

P. Sufenas Virius Lupus is a metagender, and the Doctor, Magistratum, Mystagogos, Sacerdos, and one of the founding members of the Ekklesía Antínoou — a queer, Graeco-Roman-Egyptian syncretist reconstructionist polytheist group dedicated to Antinous, the deified lover of the Roman Emperor Hadrian, and related deities and divine figures–as well as a contributing member of Neos Alexandria and a practicing Celtic Reconstructionist pagan in the traditions of gentlidecht and filidecht, as well as Romano-British, Welsh, and Gaulish deity devotions. Lupus is also dedicated to several land spirits around the area of North Puget Sound and its islands. Lupus' work (poetry, fiction, and essays) has appeared in a number of *Bibliotheca Alexandrina* devotional volumes, as well as Ruby Sara's anthologies *Datura* (2010) and *Mandragora* (2012), Inanna Gabriel and C. Bryan Brown's *Etched Offer-*

ings (2011), Lee Harrington's *Spirit of Desire: Personal Explorations of Sacred Kink* (2010), and Galina Krasskova's *When the Lion Roars* (2011). Lupus has also written several full-length books, including *The Phillupic Hymns* (2008), *The Syncretisms of Antinous* (2010), *Devotio Antinoo: The Doctor's Notes*, Volume One (2011), *All-Soul, All-Body, All-Love, All-Power: A TransMythology* (2012), *A Garland for Polydeukion* (2012), and *A Serpent Path Primer* (2012), with more on the way.

Lupus writes the "Queer I Stand" column at Patheos.com's Pagan Portal, the "Gentlidecht" blog at PaganSquare, and also blogs at Aedicula Antinoi (http://aediculaantinoi.wordpress.com/).

Lykeia opted not to provide a biography.

Jen McConnel was born and raised in Michigan, but now makes her home in North Carolina. She is a devotee of Isis, but works closely with a number of goddesses. She's been published in *Sagewoman* and *PanGaia*, and she blogs at Witches and Pagans and Patheos. *Goddess Spells for Busy Girls*, her first nonfiction title, is now available from *Weiser Books*. Visit her online at www.jenmcconnel.com.

Dr. John "Apollonius" Opsopaus has practiced magic and divination since the 1960s, during which time he has studied theurgy and other ancient forms of magic, tarot and other divination systems,

Pythagoreanism and other esoteric disciplines, and spiritual alchemy. His fiction (hymns, poetry, and prose) and nonfiction (rituals, translations, divination systems, essays) have been published in various magical and Neopagan magazines (over thirty publications). Based on his research he designed the *Pythagorean Tarot* and wrote the comprehensive *Guide to the Pythagorean Tarot* (*Llewellyn*, 2001). He presents workshops on Hellenic magic and Neopaganism, Pythagorean theurgy and spiritual practices, divination, and related topics.

Opsopaus has been involved in the magical and Neopagan communities on-line for twenty years, and his Biblioteca Arcana website (omphalos.org/BA) has won numerous awards and is featured in several Internet guides. In the early 1990s he founded the Omphalos, a networking organization for Neopagans in the Greek and Roman Traditions and one of the first internet resources especially for them.

Opsopaus is past coordinator of the Scholars Guild for the Church of All Worlds, past Arkhon of the Hellenic Kin of ADF (A Druid Fellowship), and Dean of the Department of Ceremonial Magick of the Grey School of Wizardry. Opsopaus is a member of the Grey Council and is listed under "Who's Who in the Wiccan Community" in Gerina Dunwich's *Wicca Source Book* (Citadel, 1996).

C.J. Prince, author and poet, found the Muse on the sandy shores of Summerland when she was in fourth grade. She's been writing ever since: high school and college newspapers, magazines. She was a reporter in Colorado for eighteen years, has written stage and TV scripts plus a screen play and is the author of Canvas Angels, a novel included in *Catching My Breath*. She is included in several anthologies including *Leaning into the Wind: Women Write from the Heart of the West*. She was the executive director of the Womyn's Centre of Elbert County, Colorado, for five years. She has facilitated many women's groups. She was an actress and performer for twenty-two years, and has traveled from London to Hong Kong. Now back on the west coast, she has found her soul home in the Pacific Northwest. C.J Prince lives with her husband Michael E. Berg, two Papillons, Beamer and Zee, and one rescued orange marmalade tabby, Hamilton. You can find her on Facebook under Hamilton Prince.

Juli D. Revezzo is a Florida girl, with a love of fantasy, science fiction, and Arthurian legend, so much so she gained a B.A. in English and American Literature. She loves writing stories with fantastical elements whether it be a full-on fantasy, or a story set in this world–slightly askew. She has been published in short form in *Eternal Haunted Summer*, *Crossing the River: An Anthology In Honor of Sa-*

cred Journeys, *Dark Things II: Cat Crimes* (a charity anthology for cat related charities), *Luna Station Quarterly*, *The Scribing Ibis: An Anthology of Pagan Fiction in Honor of Thoth*, and *Twisted Dreams Magazine*. She is author of *The Artist's Inheritance*, *Caitlin's Book of Shadows* and *Drawing Down the Shades* (part of the *Antique Magic* series) and has recently released her debut paranormal romance novel, *Passion's Sacred Dance*. She also has an article and book review or two out there. But her heart lies in the storytelling. She is a member of the Independent Author Network and the Magic Appreciation Tour. You can find out more about her at: http://julidrevezzo.com

Romany Rivers is a British Pagan Priestess and Reiki Master residing in Nova Scotia, Canada, where she offers support to local and online communities. Author of *Poison Pen Letters to Myself* and *The Woven Word*. The "Invocation to Demeter" is taken from *The Woven Word*.

K.S. Roy (also known as Khryseis Astra) is an artist, astrologer and writer living in Western Pennsylvania. She is particularly devoted to Hekate, Hermes, Persephone, Apollon and the Muses. She has been the Graphic Designer for *He Epistole*, a Hellenic Polytheist newsletter issued by Neokoroi, the editor for *Guardian of the Road: A Devotional*

Anthology in Honor of Hermes and is currently at work on a devotional art series for the Theoi.

Sannion is a drunken and mad vagabond priest of Dionysos. He also writes, and has published numerous books through *Nysa Press*. He plans to conquer the world, but is easily distracted so that may never happen.

Although not the original Diotima, the author does agree that the western world has invested far too much energy into separating the inseparable duo of mind and heart. **Diotima Sophia** has written widely on a number of subjects, including essays, fiction and poetry. Two of her latest books have been published by the *Bibliotheca Alexandrina*: *Dancing God* — a collection of poetry, and *Goat Foot God*, an examination of the Great God Pan; both available through Neos Alexandria (http://www.neosalexandria.org/publishing.htm). Her latest work of fiction is *Tales in Vein*, a series of short stories available in ebook and audio book format from Amazon. Her website can be found at: http://diotima-sophia.com/.

Maya Spector is a storyteller, poet, ritualist, retired children's librarian, and certified SoulCollage® facilitator. She is a life-long devotee of Persephone and Demeter and has presented several series of rituals for women based on the Persephone myth. Her poems have been published in *Queen of the Sacred Way*, *Red Thread Gold Thread: The Poet's Voice*, and *Talking To Goddess*. More of her writings and information about her ritual work can be found at: www.barryandmayaspector.com.

Charles Stein (born 1944 in New York City) is the author of thirteen books of poetry including *Views From Tornado Island* (forthcoming from *Spuyten Duyvil*), a new verse translation of *The Odyssey* (*North Atlantic Books*), *From Mimir's Head* (*Station Hill Press*), and *The Hat Rack Tree* (*Station Hill Press*). His prose writings include a vision of the Eleusinian Mysteries, *Persephone Unveiled* (*North Atlantic Books*), a critical study of poet Charles Olson's use of the writing of C.G. Jung, *The Secret of the Black Chrysanthemum* (*Station Hill Press*), and a collaborative study with George Quasha of the work of Gary Hill, *An Art of Limina: Gary Hill's Works & Writings, Ediciones Poligrafa*. He holds a Ph.D. in literature from the University of Connecticut at Storrs and lives with guitarist, choral director, and research historian, Megan Hastie in Barrytown New York. His work can be sampled at his website: www.charlessteinpoet.com.

Kate Taylor has been fascinated by Greek mythology for as long as she's been able read (and has the picture books to prove it). Now in her twenties she writes retellings of the myths in order to understand them better and is specifically devoted to Demeter. She also has a BA in English Literature and Creative Writing and an MRes in Creative Writing and her fiction and poetry has appeared in *Luna Station Quarterly*, *Eternal Haunted Summer* and published by *Paizo* and *Northumbria University Press*.

Lauren C. Teffeau was born and raised on the East Coast, educated in the South, employed in the Midwest, and now lives and dreams in the Southwest. Her work can be found in a wide variety of speculative fiction magazines and anthologies. She's a graduate of the 2012 Taos Toolbox writers workshop, and she blogs about the writing life at http://laurencteffeau.com.

Suz Thackston is a Hellenic Polytheist and ceremonial magician who lives on a small would-be farm in Western Maryland with one patient husband, a disobedient dog, two old mares, too many cats and a host of spirits. She is a homeschool mom of now-grown kids, a part-time teacher, a disorganized hausfrau, a good horsewoman, an aspiring gardener, an impractical dreamer, and an endlessly fascinated student of the world, the universe, and everything.

John J. Trause, the Director of Oradell Public Library, is the author of Eye Candy for Andy (*13 Most Beautiful... Poems for Andy Warhol's Screen Tests, Finishing Line Press*, 2013); *Inside Out, Upside*

Down, and Round and Round (*Nirala Publications*, 2012); the chapbook *Seriously Serial* (*Poets Wear Prada*, 2007; rev. ed. 2014); and *Latter-Day Litany* (*Éditions élastiques*, 1996), the latter staged Off-Off Broadway. His translations, poetry, and visual work appear internationally in many journals and anthologies, including the artists' periodical *Crossings*, the Dada journal *Maintenunt*, the journal *Offerta Speciale*, the *Uphook Press* anthologies *Hell Strung* and *Crooked* and *-gape-seed-*, and the Great Weather for Media anthology *It's Animal but Merciful*. He has shared the stage with Steven Van Zandt, Anne Waldman, Karen Finley, and Jerome Rothenberg, the page with Lita Hornick, William Carlos Williams, Woody Allen, Ted Kooser, and Pope John Paul II, and the cage with the Cumaean Sibyl, Ezra Pound, Hannibal Lector, Andrei Chikatilo, and George "The Animal" Steele. He is a founder of the William Carlos Williams Poetry Cooperative in Rutherford, N. J., and the former host and curator of its monthly reading series. He has been nominated for the Pushcart Prize (2009 – 2011, 2013).

Rosanna E. Tufts woke up one morning, having just had a dream about a Broadway Musical which would require the heroine to be tied-up for half of the show. Once she realized this was the basis for the rock opera *The Passion of Persephone*, she immediately knew that Act 1 would end with Demeter's rage aria, "Let Winter Last for Aye!" It was performed at a work-in-progress at the 2008 Capitol Fringe Festival. Videos of "Winter" and other highlights from the show are on YouTube (type "Passion of Persephone" in the search box). Rosanna has a Master of Music from Baltimore's Peabody Institute, and is the host of a weekly internet radio show, "The Tufts Get Going!" For more information about the show, see www.passionofpersephone.com. Contact Rosanna at rosanna-108@comcast.net, www.RosannaTufts.com, or www.RewriteYourStars.com.

Marian Weaver is a poet, blogger and witch with chaote leanings and a passionate interest in queer rights, freedom of religion, politics, and sex positivity. When she has time, she reads avidly. Currently, she is working on devotional poetry cycles to Ariadne, Medea, Psyche, Penelope, and Athena. Her devotional poetry to Hekate and Persephone appeared in the anthologies *Bearing Torches* and *Queen of the Sacred Way,* respectively.

Dana Wright has always had a fascination with things that go bump in the night. She is often found playing at local bookstores, trying not to maim herself with crochet hooks or knitting needles, watching monster movies with her husband and furry kids, or blogging about books. More commonly, she is chained to her computers, writing like a woman possessed. She is currently working on several children's books, young adult fiction, and horror short stories, and is trying her hand at poetry. She is a contributing author to *Siren's Call* E-zine in their "Women In Horror" issue in February 2013 and "Revenge" in October 2013, a contributing author to *Potatoes!* (upcoming), *Fossil Lake Anthology*, a top secret anthology project from *Horrified Press* due out in 2014, *Wonderstruck, Shifters: A Charity Anthology, Holiday Horrors* and the *Roms, Bombs and Zoms* anthology from *Evil Girlfriend Media*. Dana also reviews music for New Age Music Reviews, Progressive Rock Talk.com and Write a Music Review.com specializing in New Age and alternative music. She has been a contributing writer to Muzikreviews.com, *Eternal Haunted Summer, Nightmare Illustrated, Massacre Magazine, Pagan Living Magazine, The Were Traveler* October 2013 edition "The Little Magazine of Magnificent Monsters," and the December 2013 issue of *The Day the Zombies Ruled the Earth*.

Chryss Yost's poems have previously appeared in *The Hudson Review, Crab Orchard Review, Quarterly West, Solo, Askew*, and many other journals and anthologies. She was recently awarded the 2013 Patricia Dobler Award. She is co-editor of *California Poetry: From the Gold Rush to the Present* (with Dana Gioia and Jack Hicks) and *Poetry Daily: A Year of Poems from the World's Most Popular Po-*

etry Website (with Don Selby and Diane Boller). She is currently the Poet Laureate of Santa Barbara.

About Bibliotheca Alexandrina

Ptolemy Soter, the first Makedonian ruler of Egypt, established the library at Alexandria to collect all of the world's learning in a single place. His scholars compiled definitive editions of the Classics, translated important foreign texts into Greek, and made monumental strides in science, mathematics, philosophy and literature. By some accounts over a million scrolls were housed in the famed library, and though it has long since perished due to the ravages of war, fire, and human ignorance, the image of this great institution has remained as a powerful inspiration down through the centuries.

To help promote the revival of traditional polytheistic religions we have launched a series of books dedicated to the ancient gods of Greece and Egypt. The library is a collaborative effort drawing on the combined resources of the different elements within the modern Hellenic and Kemetic communities, in the hope that we can come together to praise our gods and share our diverse understandings, experiences and approaches to the divine.

A list of our current and forthcoming titles can be found on the following page. For more information on the Bibliotheca, our submission requirements for upcoming devotionals, or to learn about our organization, please visit us at neosalexandria.org.

Sincerely,

The Editorial Board of the Library of Neos Alexandria

<u>Current Titles</u>

Written in Wine: A Devotional Anthology for Dionysos

Dancing God: Poetry of Myths and Magicks

Goat Foot God

Longing for Wisdom: The Message of the Maxims

The Phillupic Hymns

Unbound: A Devotional Anthology for Artemis

Waters of Life: A Devotional Anthology for Isis and Serapis

Bearing Torches: A Devotional Anthology for Hekate

Queen of the Great Below: An Anthology in Honor of Ereshkigal

From Cave to Sky: A Devotional Anthology in Honor of Zeus

Out of Arcadia: A Devotional Anthology for Pan

Anointed: A Devotional Anthology for the Deities of the Near and Middle East

The Scribing Ibis: An Anthology of Pagan Fiction in Honor of Thoth

Queen of the Sacred Way: A Devotional Anthology in Honor of Persephone

Unto Herself: A Devotional Anthology for Independent Goddesses

The Shining Cities: An Anthology of Pagan Science Fiction

Guardian of the Road: A Devotional Anthology in Honor of Hermes

Harnessing Fire: A Devotional Anthology in Honor of Hephaestus

Beyond the Pillars: An Anthology of Pagan Fantasy

Queen of Olympos: A Devotional Anthology for Hera and Iuno

A Mantle of Stars: A Devotional Anthology in Honor of the Queen of Heaven

Crossing the River: An Anthology in Honor of Sacred Journeys

Ferryman of Souls: A Devotional for Charon

Potnia: An Anthology in Honor of Demeter

<u>Forthcoming Titles</u>

The Queen of the Sky Who Rules Over All the Gods: A Devotional Anthology in Honor of Bast

Daughter of the Sun: A Devotional Anthology in Honor of Sekhmet

Seasons of Grace: A Devotional in Honor of the Mousai, the Charites, and the Horae

From the Roaring Deep: A Devotional for Poseidon and the Spirits of the Sea

Shield of Wisdom: A Devotional Anthology in Honor of Athena

Megaloi Theoi: A Devotional Anthology for the Dioskouroi and Their Families

Sirius Rising: A Devotional Anthology for Cyno-cephalic Deities

Printed in Poland
by Amazon Fulfillment
Poland Sp. z o.o., Wrocław